Practical

Kos
and neighbouring islands

1994
Hayit Publishing

Current practical information is essintial for a quality travel guide. Although every effort was made during our research to keep this guide up to date, prices and other information can change rapidly — sometimes within weeks. For this reason, we would be grateful for any comments, suggestions or information you might have concerning the island of Kos.
Hayit Publishing, c/o Amalgamated Book Services Ltd., Suite 1, Royal Star Arcade, High Street, Maidstone, Kent ME 14 1JL.

1st Edition 1994
ISBN: 1 874251 22 3

© copyright 1994 for the English version: Hayit Publishing, GB, Ltd, London/England
© copyright 1990, 1992, 1993, 1994 for the original version: Hayit Verlag, Cologne, Germany

Author: Kurt Bartzke
Editorial Assistant: Klaus Eckhardt
Translation: Dagmar Gabrio
Revision, Adaption: Scott Reznik
Typesetting: Anglia Marketing, Cologne/Germany
Print: Sutter & Partner, Essen/Germany
Cover Photo: TransGlobe Agency
Photography: Rainer Skrovny: pages 15, 51, 67, 74, 79, 103, 107; Dr. Kurt Seidl: pages 54, 86, 106; Christina Pannhausen: page 11; Touropa Bildarchiv: page 111; Kurt Bartzke, Greek Centre for Tourism, Intercontinental Reisen, Peter Kanzler, orion interconti Touristik, Karsten zur Nieden
Maps: Ralf Tito: pages 2 and 3
      Gerd Oberländer: page 58
Sketches: Gerd Oberländer: pages 14, 62, 63

2.3/Gd/Sr//Sr

All rights reserved   Printed in Germany

Using this book

Books in the **Practical Travel** series offer a wealth of practical information. You will find the most important tips for your travels conviniently arranged in alphabetical order.

Cross-references aid in orientation so that even entries which are not covered in depth, for instance "Holiday Apartments" lead you to the appropriate entry, in this case "Accommodation". Also thematically altered entries are also cross-referenced. For example, under the heading "Medication", there appears the reference "Medical Care", "Pharmacies" and "Vaccinations".

With practical travel guides from the **Practical Travel** series, the information is already available before you depart on your trip. Thus, you are already familiar with necessary travel documents and maps, even customs regualtions. Travel within the country is made easier through comprehensive presentation of public transportation, car rentals in addition to the practical tips ranging from medical assistance to newspapers available in the country. The descriptions of cities are arranged alphabetically as well and include the most important significant sights. In addition, these entries include a wealth of practical tips — from shopping, restaurants and accommodation to important local addresses. Background information does not come up short either. You will find interesting information about the people and their culture as well as the regional geography, history and current political and economic situation.

As a particular service to our readers, **Practical Travel** includes prices in hard currencies to provide a more accurate impression of prices, even in countries with high rates of inflation. Most prices quoted in this book have been converted to US$ and £.

Kos — steeped in history and sunshine

In spring, the landscapes of Kos explode in colour — a sea of flowers blankets the island. This is the perfect season do discover what the island has to offer on foot.

This island in the Dodecanese group of Greek islands has a history which goes back well before the birth of Christ. Ancient ruins can be found in abundance on Kos, the most famous of which is most certainly the Asclepius Sanctuary. The cradle of modern medicine, Kos was the home and workplace of the famous ancient Greek physician Hippocrates who brought world fame to the Asclepius Sanctuary. Today, these impressive ruins can be toured as can numerous archaeological excavations in Kos City. These were unearthed resulting from a devastating earthquake — a tragic event that did have its beneficial aspects in this respect. Kos City itself is a hybrid of the ancient and the modern, where remnants of the turbulent past can be seen on every street corner. But by no means is the city old and lifeless — having meanwhile adapted to tourism, Kos City has everything one could desire yet has managed to preserve its own special charm.

Those more interested in a holiday on the beach will find seemingly endless beaches, some perfect for swimming and others with ideal conditions for windsurfing.

And if that isn't enough, Kos also makes an ideal point of departure for excursions to discover what other islands in this region of the Aegean have to offer. Greece has always had a special relationship with the sea beginning with Odysseus' voyages in ancient times and continuing up to present with excellent ferry connections to neighbouring islands. Whether its Astipálea with the beautiful towns of Skála and Chóra, Kálymnos with its port city of Póthia, Symi, one of the most beautiful Dodecanese islands, or even Turkey, one should definitely plan in ample time to island hop, adding diversity to the holiday experience.

Contents

Registry of Places

Agios Fokás 9
Agios Stéfanos 10
Andimáchia 11
Asfendioú 13
Asclepius Sanctuary 13
Astipálea (excursion) 16
Bodrum / Halikarnassós
  (excursion)....................... 21
Díkeos 32
Eleón 33
Kálymnos (excursion) 46
Kamári 52
Kardámaena 53
Kéfalos 56
Kos City 57
Lámbi 73
Léros (excursion) 76
Linopótis 83
Marmári 84
Mastichári 84
Nísyros (excursion) 89
Palaiópyli (Old Pylí) 95
Pátmos (excursion) 95
Psérimos (excursion) 105
Pylí 106
Symi (excursion) 112
Tílos (excursion) 116
Tingáki 117
Tolári 118
Turkey (excursion) 125
Zía 128
Zipári 128

General Information

Accommodation 9
Animals and Wildlife 12
Automobile Clubs 20
Beaches 20
Camping 22
Car Rental 22
Children 23
Climate 24
Clothing 26
Conduct 26
Crime 26
Cuisine 27
Customs Regulations 31
Discounts 32
Economy 32
Electricity 33
Embassies 34
Entertainment 34
Equipment 35
Fuel 35
Geography 36
Greetings 37
Health Insurance 37
Hippocrates 37
History 39
Holidays and Celebratons .. 42
Icons 44
Insurance 45
Kafenío 46
Language 75
Maps 84
Medical Care 85

Monasteries 86	Sponges 110
Money 87	Sports and Recreation 111
Mythology 88	Telephones 115
Nudism 94	Time of Day 117
Olympic Airways 94	Tourist Information 118
The People of Kos 101	Traffic Regulations 118
Períptero 103	Travel Documents 120
Pharmacies 104	Travel on Kos 120
Photography/Video 104	Travelling to Kos 124
Postal System 105	Vegetation 125
Religion 107	Visas 127
Shopping 109	Weights and Measures 127
Sights 109	
Speed Limits 110	Wine 127

Accommodation

All **hotels** on Kos are subject to a classification ranging from luxurious to categories A to E. However, it is sometimes hard to make out the exact differences, especially when dealing with the lower categories. Thus, it is not always true that a hotel in a higher category is more expensive than its counterpart which ranks in a lower category but provides more comfort. The advantage of this classification for holidaymakers is that prices are fixed and must be posted in public (usually in the rooms).

However, do not be confused by these lists: the exact price of the room is stated but there is still the possibly of surcharges for a number of special services. It is best to ask at the reception for the exact price of these additional services.

It is also possible that the price posted is merely a basis for bargaining on which discounts are possible, for example in the early or off-season when hotel capacity is only half filled.

The numerous **guest houses** and **"rent rooms",** the second largest contingent of accommodation, are less regulated and less often subject to price control. Here, it has become almost customary to negotiate the price. However, it is recommended to be skeptical and if in doubt, to check with the local tourism authorities since there are unfortunately "black sheep" among the proprietors.

There are no **youth hostels** on Kos but the very simple guest houses do offer accommodation at prices equally low.

Holiday apartments can be rented before the trip and on the spot by many agencies or the → *Tourist Information Office*. Bookings on Kos are generally slightly less expensive. The same applies to **holiday houses**. Nevertheless, the nicest form of accommodation are **private rooms,** offering the opportunity to experience the country and its people close up.

Agios Fokás

Agios Fokás is a cape south east of Kos City. The coastline here becomes increasingly steep and includes some very nice, small bays for swimming. In this especially beautiful landscape, a number of new hotels are being built.

A rather unpleasant road leads from here to the island's old *thermal baths* at a distance of only three kilometres (2 miles). Everything here seems a bit run-down and neglected. The small gravel beach is an inviting spot for a swim and the tavern also makes a pleasant stop.

Agios Stéfanos

Agios Stéfanos are the remnants of two early Christian churches situated directly on the bay of Kéfalos.

These are the most well-preserved of all churches on the island and are therefore worth seeing.

The typical floor Dodecanese mosaics with birds and other motives are very beautiful and also well preserved.

Agios Stéfanos is said to have been founded in the 5th century AD.

Even the animals retreat into the shade to escape the midday heat

Andimáchia

Andimáchia is located about 25 kilometres (16 miles) from Kos City in the island's interior. It can accredit most of its renown to the international airport in its direct vicinity.

Andimáchia is a typically Greek provincial village, which has enjoyed some economic upswing but apart from that, has not profited from the boom in tourism on Kos being only a place to pass through.

Andimáchia is situated in Kos' main agricultural region with vineyards and vegetable fields extending to the north of town. Those who decide to stay here have the choice between the beaches on the northern coast near → *Mastichári* or those on the southern coast near → *Kardámaena* because the distance to both places is almost the same. There are no sights worth mentioning in Andimáchia but are the ruins of the fort of the → *Andimáchia Fort (see below)* are located nearby. The town has a post office, an OTE, and a bank.

A typical scene on Kos...

Accommodation: Several hotels and guest houses offer accommodation for tourists.
Transportation: The town is accessible by bus from Kos City operation several times daily.

Andimáchia / **Fortress**

The fortress of Andimáchia is situated about 3 kilometres (2 miles) from the town itself and can be reached via a narrow and dusty road. The fort was built in the 14th century AD and will impress visitors through its enormous dimensions. Unfortunately, it has fallen victim to decay to a large degree so that it is more the location and relative seclusion that make a visit worthwhile.

Animals and Wildlife

Unfortunately, the wealth of species among Kos' wildlife cannot compare to the diversity of plant life on the island. On isolated occasions, especially in forest regions, one might be able to see some larger animals such as *wild boars* or *foxes;* much more frequent, however, are *rabbits, pheasants,* and *partridges.*

In rocky areas, stones may conceal *scorpions.* Their stings are not terribly dangerous but are extremely painful, making it wise to wear sturdy shoes when walking outside.

There are also *snakes* on Kos but one will only be able to see them on very rare occasions since they are very timid animals. Although the bite of a sand viper is quite dangerous, visitors will probably not meet up with any of these animals if cautious while outside.

The numerous *flocks of sheep and goats* are a problem for many islands because, given their continual and hearty appetite for fresh green plants, no new vegetation can take root.

One will probably see *lizards* such as *geckos* quite often when they sunbathe on the warm stones. These are completely harmless and entertaining animals that might only be a bit frightening at first due to their unusual size and colour.

Asfendioú

Asfendioú is probably one of the most affluent villages on the island, situated in the lush green of the → *Díkeos Mountain's* northern slope. The inhabitants live mainly from agriculture. Asfendioú actually consists of various small and very small mountain villages which have been incorporated into one town.

Asfendioú is a typical farmer's village where the island's tourism seems to have passed by, leaving almost no trace. The view from this vantage point extends over the numerous fertile fields on the plain of Kos to the islands of → *Psérimos* and → *Kálymnos*.

Most fields on this fertile plain belong to the farmers of Asfendioú. They live there in small summer houses; in winter, they return to the main village.

Accommodation: Up to present, there is no accommodation in the form of private rooms in Asfendioú.

Transportation: The bus from Kos City operates once daily.

This town also makes a good point of departure for very nice walking tours through the various mountain villages with the opportunity to return by bus from Pylí.

Asclepius Sanctuary

The Asclepius Sanctuary is the most famous sight on Kos and the most important one in the entire Dodecanese. Situated some 4 kilometres (2½ miles) from Kos City near the small village of Platáni, it can be reached very easily using all types of transportation.

The temple complex is open daily from 8 am to 3 pm; closed Mondays. Admission is around £1.10 ($1.90). The visitor will seldom have a similar opportunity to see a complex such as this which merges so well with the countryside as is the case with the Aesclepius Sanctuary. The view over the plain seems to never end, extending across the plain to the island's capital and on to the coast of Asia Minor. One can perceive the inspiration this landscape must have evoked in the former builders of the Asclepius Sanctuary.

ASCLEPIUS SANCTUARY

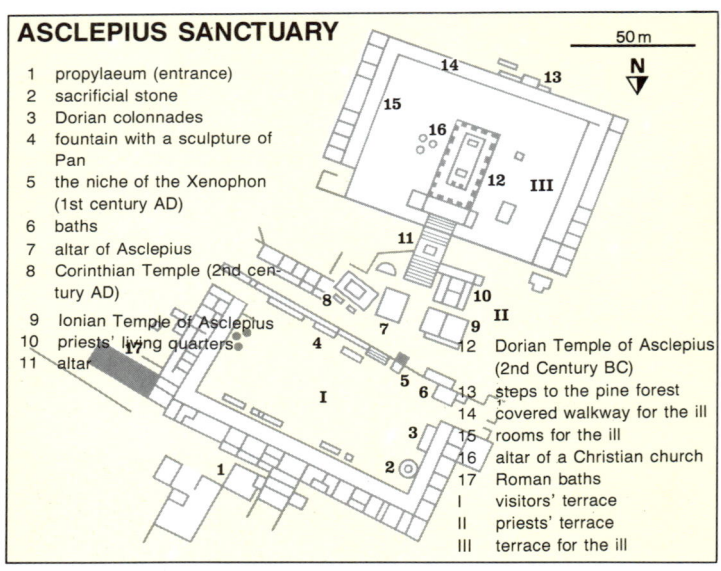

1. propylaeum (entrance)
2. sacrificial stone
3. Dorian colonnades
4. fountain with a sculpture of Pan
5. the niche of the Xenophon (1st century AD)
6. baths
7. altar of Asclepius
8. Corinthian Temple (2nd century AD)
9. Ionian Temple of Asclepius
10. priests' living quarters
11. altar
12. Dorian Temple of Asclepius (2nd Century BC)
13. steps to the pine forest
14. covered walkway for the ill
15. rooms for the ill
16. altar of a Christian church
17. Roman baths
I. visitors' terrace
II. priests' terrace
III. terrace for the ill

The Sanctuary was discovered in 1902 by the German archaeologist Herzog who started excavations which would be continued in 1933 by the Italians.

In the 4th century BC, the sanctuary was at the height of its importance when the famous physician → *Hippocrates* extended it, making it one of the largest medical centres in the world during that time.

However, it was after his death that Hippocrates' teachings and healing arts were put into practice, contributing to the reputation of excellence that the island of Kos enjoyed throughout the world during Antiquity.

The Asclepius cult had already been brought to the island in the 9th century BC by Dorian immigrants but only gained true importance and influence in the 5th and 4th century BC. Asclepius was worshipped as the son of Apollo and was said to have been able to heal people from their ailments.

The entire Asclepius Sanctuary dates back to the 3rd century BC and consists of three terraces above each other connected by broad stairways.

On the lowest terrace, one could find buildings with treatment and healing rooms. It was here where sulphurous water flowed from small fountains. The terraces were bordered on three sides by colonnades, comparable to a lobby or foyer.

The second terrace was used in worshipping the gods. The small Asclepius altar was situated here, which was said to have contained all the treasures of the sanctuary. A second altar dedicated to Apollo could also be found on this terrace.

The third terrace has ruins of the Dorian temple, the large Asclepius temple from the 2nd century BC. In the centuries to follow, it was

In 1902, the Asclepius Sanctuary was discovered by the German Archaeologist Herzog

converted to a church dedicated to the Virgin Mary. Colonnades used as halls for the ill could be found here as well. Much more interesting, however, is the view from this vantage point over the lower terraces of the complex and down across the plain of Kos. The former "holy grove" begins beyond the third terrace and is a large pine forest — an inviting setting for long walks.

Astipálea *(Excursion)*

When thinking about it, it is not terribly clear why Astipálea is considered part of the Dodecanese since the island is located quite a distance away in the Aegean Sea. Coupled with this, the residents feel much more a part of the Cyclades. Situated east of Amorgós, Astipálea constitutes a small world of its own; yet, it is has also made the acquaintance of tourism.

Astipálea is the driest and most barren island in the Aegean Sea; only the valley of Livádia is a green oasis in the middle of bare landscape.

Day trips to Astipálea are offered from Kos but one should really consider the option spending several days on the island, considering the long trip there.

There are not many sights, but the location of the coastal village of Chóra is enticing.

Apart from that, Astipálea is very well suited for quiet and relaxing holidays; it has nice small, gravel bays and very clean water with a rugged coastline.

Astipálea / **The Towns of Skála and Chóra**

The most important settlements on the island are **Skála** and **Chóra,** both confronting arriving visitors with a rather strange sight. The port city Skála's snow-white houses are clustered in front of the bare, brown rocks of the island; somewhat above, just below the abandoned castle, Chóra's (Chóra = city) houses are seemingly glued to the mountain slope. Skála is the newer of the two towns which have meanwhile grown together. It is here that one will find most accommodation and most of the taverns. At the time Chóra was constructed, protection against pirate attacks was an important factor as can be seen by the layout of the town. Winding alleyways run through the village, the cubic houses are all kept in gleaming white; a very beautiful place with numerous photogenic nooks and crannies. The Platía Eleftherías forms the centre of Chóra, from which a number of roadways lead off to the old fort, where one can enjoy the beautiful panorama of portions of the island, Chóra itself and the deep blue water of the Aegean Sea.

Below the fort is the oldest part of Chóra. It is here where the *Panagía Portaítissa Church* dating back to 1764 can be found. It contains a very precious icon.

Astipálea / **Excursions on the Island**

The main beach is located below Chóra in *Livádia Valley*, within good walking distance.

Even during high season, this gravel beach is not crowded and the hinterlands seem especially beautiful with their numerous orange, lemon, and olive trees. Livádia is the island's only agricultural area worth mentioning. Some taverns at this beach provide holiday travellers with all the necessities. The rest of the island is almost entirely unexplored, only lonely donkey tracks run through it. After a walk of several hours, one can reach the *Agios Ioánnis Monastery*, situated in complete seclusion.

Another destination worth mentioning is the hamlet of **Váthys** in the eastern portions of the island, best reached by boat. There are only around a dozen people living here; in summer, the tavern offers exquisite fish dishes — almost all of the village residents are fishermen.

Near the village of **Análypsis** one can admire the remains of two Roman villas with well-preserved floor mosaics. A modest number of private rooms is available and the village also has a tavern. Nearby are several small and very charming bays well suited to swimming.

Near the village, one can also find a small airport, presently under construction. It was supposed to be completed in 1989/1990.

Astipálea / **Practical Information**

Accommodation: All hotels are located in Skála; in Chóra, almost only private accommodation is available.

Astipálea (Excursion)

C-cat: Vivamare, double room around £12 ($22), Tel: 02 42/6 13 28.
D-cat: Aegeon, double room around £8.50 ($16), Tel: 02 42/6 12 36.
D-cat: Astynea, Mih. Karageórgis 21, double room around £8.50 ($16), Tel: 02 42/6 12 09.
D-cat: Paradissos, Mih. Karageórgis 24, double-room about $16/£8.50, Tel: 02 42/6 12 24.

There is a camping area on the road to Análypsis; however, it offers only limited shade. The price per person/tent is around £2 ($3.75). Tel: 02 42/6 13 38; open from May to October.

Banks: There is a bank (open from 8 am to 2 pm), changing money is also possible in the hotels or at the travel agency.

Beaches: All beaches are gravel; the main beach is situated below Chóra on Livádia Bay. The water surrounding the island is very clear and ideal for scuba diving or snorkelling.

Kos offers a number of opportunities for excursions to neighbouring islands...

Astipálea (Excursion)

Medical Care: There is a medical practice, Tel: 02 42/6 12 22; in case of emergency, help can be requested from Kos.

Restaurants: The more beautiful and stylish taverns are in Chóra, although the ones in Skála can also be recommended. Worth more than one visit: "Psaropoula" Tavern at the Platía Eleftherías serves very good fish dishes at reasonable prices. Also highly recommended: "Kali Kardiá" Tavern at the bank near the harbour with a beautiful terrace.

Tip: The Kafenío "Oi Myloi", also situated near the harbour; time seems to have come to a standstill in this locale.

Transportation

Buses: There are two bus lines on the island serving all of the island's towns at least once a day. The bus schedules are adapted to the needs of the local residents; for example, in the morning buses run to the main villages and in the evening, back to the small villages. This might make taking a taxi necessary now and again.

but Kos itself also has a lot to offer, like the small church in Zía

Automobile Clubs

Ferries: There a ferries to Kos and Piraeus three times a week. In addition, there is an express boat to Kos and Kálymnos several times a week. For more details, ask the harbour police or at the "Gournas Tours".
Important Addresses: The harbour police is located directly at the docks, Tel: 02 42/6 12 08. There is a post office, OTE, and a bank in the village.
Tourist information and tickets are available at the "Gournas Tours" travel agency.

Automobile Clubs

The headquarters of the Greek automobile club ELPA can be found in Athens, Odós Messógion 2. Many International automobile club coverage is also accepted in Greece.
The ELPA does not have an office on Kos, but in emergencies, the tourist police in Kos City will be of assistance (Tel: 02 42/2 82 27). Generally speaking, there are only few cars from foreign countries on the island since most tourists rent cars. This has the advantage that in case of a breakdown, one can call the car rental agency.

Beaches

Kos is extremely well-suited for a holiday on the beach, offering a variety of truly exceptional, sandy beaches. The most important ones are:
Northern Coast: → *Tingáki* with long, sandy beaches and well-developed in terms of tourism; there are high waves sometimes. → *Mastichári* likewise has a very long, sandy beach, in part covered with dunes. The beach slopes off gently into the water making it well suited for children. The surf is relatively calm.
→ *Marmári* also has a beautiful, long beach.
Southern Coast: The two most beautiful beaches on Kos' southern coast are located near the settlement of → *Kardámaena* where the heavily frequented beach extends for a number of kilometres. What is certainly the most beautiful beach on the island can be found at → *Kéfalos Bay*. However, these beaches are not recommended to those seeking peace and tranquillity.

Kos City: Several small beaches extend to the east and west of Kos City; however, these are relatively crowded during the tourist season. The more beautiful areas are to the east of the city. This is also where the only camping area on the island is located (→ *Kos City / Accommodation*). Since the island is rather small on the whole and the coastline is relatively straight (→ *Geography*), secluded bays for swimming are not to be found on this island.

Bodrum / Halikarnassós (Excursion)

One of the most interesting and charming excursions is almost certainly a day-trip to the Turkish city Bodrum, opposite Kos on the Asia Minor continent.

These trips are generally organised and carried out daily — for more details see the EOT tourist information in → *Kos City* — but the tours depend a great deal on the general political situation.

Bodrum is a very picturesque harbour town and underwent an enormous upswing in recent years due to booming tourism in Turkey. Bodrum is a very lively city, yachts from all over the world fill the harbour and the harbour promenade is packed with pubs and bars.

Bodrum / **Sights**

The most famous sovereign of this city was King Mausolos, who even ordered an enormous monument to himself during his lifetime. This monument, *a mausoleum,* counted among the "seven wonders of the world" at that time. Today, there is very little left to see since most of it was destroyed by an earthquake.

The most famous landmark of the city is *St. Peter's Fortress* situated on a peninsula. It was built by crusaders during the 15th century and is well preserved. The building houses Bodrum's *museum* with interesting findings from the surrounding regions as well as a *underwater museum.* Since there is only limited time during such a day-trip to → *Turkey*, one will probably not have the opportunity to see the beautiful areas surrounding Bodrum.

Buses and Bus Connections → *Travel on Kos, individual entries*

Camping

Kos is not a typical camping island since most holiday travellers come here on package tours. For this reason, there is only one official camping area on Kos east of → *Kos City*. Despite its beautiful beaches, the island offers only very few opportunities to pitch a tent just anywhere because most beaches belong to hotels or holiday clubs which are not too fond of backpackers.

As in the whole of Greece, it is officially prohibited to pitch a tent outside a camping area on Kos as well. The reason for this is that on numerous occasions, the nature suffered severe damage by campers; a careless flick of cigarette ash can cause devastating forest fires. The Díkeos massif is still quite densely wooded and the people of Kos are very interested in keeping it that way. Therefore, the number of campers on the island is limited and even during high season, even the small camping area will have enough room.

Car Rental

The island has a number of car rental agencies, especially in Kos City and the larger tourist areas. The vehicles are not always in the condition visitors might expect; thus, a test drive is recommended. It is also worthwhile to book a car in advance since a waiting period of 2 to 3 days is not uncommon, especially during the high season. The prices are fairly high in comparison to international standards but do usually include mileage. A small vehicle in the A category (e.g. a Fiat Panda) will cost between £29 ($54) and £38 ($71) per day, £86.50 ($162) for 3 days and about £140 ($268) for 5 days.

It is generally recommended to take out supplemental personal and comprehensive insurance to cover additional costs if having caused an accident. However, even with supplemental insurance, there could still be some problems: even though all vehicles in Greece including Kos must meanwhile have liability insurance, the coverage is usually much too low and Greek insurance companies are quite often reluctant to pay promptly. Thus, the car rental agencies tend to first charge the renter. Therefore, if involved in any accident, be sure that it is registered by the police even if the other party does not insist on it.

Large international car rental agencies such as Avis or Budget have offices on Kos. These are usually somewhat more expensive than the local agencies but most certainly have more "international" standards. The addresses of local car rental agencies are listed under the individual entries in this guide.

Children

Kos is highly recommended for a holiday with children because of its numerous and, by Greek standards, good sandy beaches. Everything a child needs can be found on Kos without any problems. Even disposable nappies and baby food in jars are available, although prices are

The first view of Kos City from the ferry signals the start of an unforgetable holiday

noticeably higher. It is especially important to protect small children from the intense rays of the sun (suntan lotion with high protection factors) and children should not be fed vegetables and fruits that have not been washed beforehand. Apart from this, children should have no severe problems in adapting to the different food and climate. Very often, children have a much easier time adapting to the different conditions than adults do.

However, it is still recommended to bring along preventative or special medications. Physicians on Kos tend to quickly prescribe antibiotics even when dealing only with harmless infections.

When travelling by air as a part of a package tour, children under 4 are only charged 10% of the normal price but are not entitled to their own seat. If children sleep in an extra bed in the parent's room, hotels offer a discount between 20 and 75%, depending on the season. In most guest houses and private rooms, it is almost taken for granted that there is no extra charge for small children. Discounts on admission to museums or performances range from 50 to 100%.

When travelling with a child in Greece and on Kos, one will often be spoken to by the Greeks and easily get into conversation. No one will be annoyed at a crying child in a tavern and very often, small presents are also given to children since Greeks are very fond of children.

Climate

Like on the other islands of the Dodecanese, the weather on Kos is characterised by a typically Mediterranean climate with hot summers and mild, humid winters.

Winter usually lasts from November to March, is wet and rather unpleasant. This is the wettest period of the year but temperatures seldom fall below 10°C (50°F). Although storms sweep across the island, there are also days with spring-like weather.

Snow is very rare and can only be found on the very high mountains of Rhodes and Sámos.

April marks the beginning of the short spring season — probably the most beautiful season. The island erupts in green, brooks still contain water and the entire island is transformed into an ocean of flowers.

Rain becomes increasingly rare and there are numerous beautiful, sunny days with pleasant temperatures. The water is still too cold to swim but this season is ideal for hiking. Seemingly unannounced, the long, dry and hot summer starts in May. The sky remains almost cloudless until September; there is virtually no rainfall and temperatures climb above the 30°C (85°F) mark. Despite the heat, Kos is very pleasant in summer because the constant and cool northeasterly wind called Méltémi. Thus, the heat is astonishingly easy to bear. Even during the hottest period of the year this northeasterly wind causes clouds to form on the northern slopes of → *Díkeo Mountain* which bring along sufficient humidity. On the whole, Kos' climate is much more consistent than for example on the Cyclades.

Sometimes, the wind can whip up into a storm and paralyse all shipping traffic between the islands for several days. Even in summer, the Aegean Sea is unpredictable. In late summer, in September and October, Kos takes on a brown, burnt and dried appearance, a testimony to the summer heat. It is at this time that sea has reached its highest temperature.

Without an actual autumn, the summer directly gives way to winter in November even though swimming might still be possible in some places.

Climate Table - Average Air and Water Temperatures in °C (°F)

	Air	Water
January	12 (53.6)	14 (57.2)
February	12 (53.6)	14 (57.2)
March	13 (55.4)	14 (57.2)
April	17 (62.6)	16 (60.8)
May	20 (68)	18 (64.4)
June	24 (75.2)	21 (69.8)
July	26 (78.8)	24 (75.2)
August	26 (78.8)	25 (77)
September	24 (75.2)	22 (71.6)
October	20 (68)	20 (68)
November	17 (62.6)	16 (60.8)
December	14 (57.2)	14 (57.2)

Clothing

Kos is primarily a summer resort; however, a sweater should not be missing in anybody's luggage for the evenings, especially since the weather during the low and off-season can be rather cool. When planning on hiking, good shoes, trousers with long legs, and hats are recommended. Apart from these articles, light clothing (cotton/wool) is best suited to the climate. Due to intense rays of the sun, sunglasses should definitely be brought along. When visiting churches or monasteries respect of Greek tradition requires long trousers, a longer dress and a decent top that covers the shoulders. One should always bear in mind: the way one presents oneself determines the way one is treated by the host.

Conduct

How should a visitor behave in Greece and on Kos? Behaving as one would at home should prove adequate in most cases.
One should always bear in mind the fact that one is a guest in the country and the host country has every right to demand respect and proper conduct in return.
Being a guest means enjoying hospitality but never taking advantages of it since in many cases the guest will be much more affluent than his or her host.
The Greek word for stranger is identical with the word for guest: "o xénos". Thus, one should feel as such wherever travels may lead.. and behave appropriately.

Credit Cards → *Money*

Crime

As in many other European tourist resorts, the crime rate on Kos rises drastically during the summer season. It is especially petty theft and robberies which increase.

However, in comparison to other large international tourist areas, the crime rate on Kos remains relatively low. If certain precautions are taken, the one need not fear being robbed on the street.

If, however, one should find oneself in such a situation, it is best to contact the next police station to register a report. This is very important in settling an insurance claim. If identification or other important documents have been lost or stolen, inform the nearest embassy or consulate. They will be able to provide a temporary replacement after the theft has been reported to the local police. (→ *Embassies, Kos City / Important Addresses*).

Cuisine

Food

Greek cuisine is rather basic without refinement and characterised by the rural surroundings. It can not be compared to the Greek food served outside the country. Generally, spices are used modestly, unlike olive oil which can be found in great abundance.

Unfortunately, the food on Kos has drifted far from its origins and there are only few taverns offering good Greek food. Most taverns and restaurants have adapted to the international taste of the tourists, thus offering international cuisine with Greek nuances.

One must look quite a while for the simple rural taverns (→ *individual entries*). It is here where the guest may still enter the kitchen, take a look into pots and pans and choose their meal.

The choice of food in these taverns is usually limited to grilled dishes — *cutlets, souvlaki* etc. Other foods include *French fries* (which are unfortunately no longer hand-made from fresh potatoes) and the *Greek Salad* where the ingredients depend on the season, but always contain tomatoes and cucumbers in the summer. Olives, onions and red peppers may be other ingredients and feta cheese makes this dish into the famous "Choriátiki Salatá", or Greek farmer's salad. Usually, this salad with some bread makes for a light meal perfect for hot days. The *omelette* which can be made from eggs only or include potatoes, tomatoes or cheese is another dish which can be found everywhere. Starting the day with an omelette for breakfast is indeed a treat and will ward off hunger well into the afternoon hours. The *mezédes* small snacks served with an oúso are also worth mentioning. Meanwhile, *fish* has become far less common in Greece and on the islands since overfishing has begun to show its effects in the Aegean and eastern Mediterranean. Now, fish is among the most expensive dishes on Greek menus. Kos has to import in part large amounts of fish from France, Spain and even from Japan.

One should bear in mind that restaurants never indicate the prices for a serving of fish but are prices per kilo. Generally speaking, the guests themselves choose the fish, the fish is then weighed and the price is stated.

Whether grilled, fried, or cooked — fish in Greek restaurants is always a delicacy. It is not always true that the most expensive fish are the best (for example, the Barbúnia, a reddish sea barbel); the less expensive fish are also very tasty. Fish of lesser quality are often used to make the so-called "Psarósoupa", a kind of *fish soup* similar to French Bouillabaisse. Those who are not scared off by an occasional fish bone should try it. The "Estiatória", the restaurants, offer a greater variety of dishes. Apart from grilled dishes, they offer a number of prepared dishes, mostly *casseroles*, which are kept in steam tables. Some of these dishes are vegetarian or prepared with minced meat, such as pastitsio — a casserole with noodles; moussaka — a casserole with potatoes, aubergines and minced meat; as well as other vegetable casseroles, all very reasonably priced.

The dishes are only really hot or at least warm at lunchtime. In the afternoon or evening, they are only slightly warm. This is very typical for Greek preferences and it is often said that this is the best way for the spices to develop their full flavour. However, the real reason for this is that the houses and taverns did not have an oven of their own earlier and had to cook all the food at the baker's. It is no surprise that the foods were only slightly warm when they finally arrived at home.

Those who want to be sure that the food is freshly prepared and hot should not be shy and ask directly if the food has been prepared on that day ("apó símera") and if it is still hot ("sésti").

However, in more recent years, fast food is becoming increasingly popular on Kos, whether it be sandwiches or hamburgers. Pizzerias and gyros stands sprout up like mushrooms on the island — a concession to the increase in tourists.

On the other hand, why should the drastic changes in eating habits which can be observed in many other countries stop at the gates of Greece? Just because we might think hamburgers and sirtaki do not fit together?

Beverages

Greece's national drink is neither wine nor beer but a good glass of fresh cool water. Water is still served without asking in all taverns or kafenía frequented by local residents. It can be drunk without reservation everywhere.

A meal is, of course, accompanied by *wine*. Most red, white and rosé wines are quite dry and therefore best as table wines. The *retsina,* a resin table wine is not to everyone's taste but after having gotten used to its unusual flavour, many cannot do without it. As wines go, retsina is very palatable and smooth.

With regard to *oúso,* one should take care to either mix it with sufficient water or have it along with a snack. Formerly, oúso was always served with small snacks (so-called "mezédes"), for example olives, cucumber slices, nuts or, as common along the coast, small pieces of octopus. However, this pleasant gesture has all but died out all over Greece and of course on Kos since tourists drink oúso all by itself.

Beer is well on its way to replace wine as a drink with the meal and some beer brands are brewed under licence in Greece (e.g. Amstel, Henninger, Löwenbräu, Heinecken). The beer does not taste bad but it is brewed with less alcohol and is fairly expensive by Greek standards.

In regard to *coffee,* the Greeks differentiate between Greek coffee and instant coffee. The instant coffee served cold is called "frappé" and is an excellent thirst quencher.

Greek coffee is served in many variations, almost always accompanied by a glass of water. The three typical variations are: "skéto" = without sugar, "métrio" = half sweet, "glikó" = sweet and "dipló" = double portion. Greek coffee is always served without milk.

In a bar or restaurant

How does the foreign guest behave in a Greek bar or restaurant? Of course, it is always best to do as the locals and call the waiter with a polite hiss. Otherwise, one could spend the entire evening at a table without being served. In simple taverns, it is recommend to ask to see the kitchen or simply go there without being asked. Here, one can choose a meal. One should bear in mind that for each dish chosen, a full portion is served and all of the dishes are brought at the same time. This can easily become too much for even the most hearty eaters. A better option is to order less at first and then order more if need be which is customary in Greek restaurants.

Tipping is customary and expected. The "mikrós" (often a child bringing bread, knives and forks and clearing the table afterwards) should by no means be forgotten since tips are quite often their only income. Unfortunately, child labour is an everyday occurance in Greek restaurants.

Whiling away the time at a tavern, one can enjoy the vew of Kéfalos Bay for hours on end

Tip: The best bars and restaurants can be recognised in that they are frequented by many locals. It is often the case that these places do not have flashy neon signs.

Customs Regulations

Upon entry, there are no customs limitations on articles for personal use or for gifts with a value up to 70,000 drachmas (= about £220/$413). Furthermore, no duty is charged on 300 cigarettes or 75 cigars or 150 cigarillos or 400 grams of tobacco as well as matches, 5 litres of alcohol under 22 % (such as beer and wine), 1½ litres of spirits, 75 grams of perfume and ⅜ litres of cologne. When shopping in duty-free shops, the following amounts are allowed: 2 litres of wine or 1 litre of spirits, 200 cigarettes or 100 cigarillos, 50 grams of perfume. However, it can be expeced that these regulations are subject to change upon implementation of the European common market.

When entering the country by car, this is noted in one's passport and checked when leaving the country. If the car is not taken back, rather substantial import taxes are levied (therefore, always make sure to get written confirmation from the local police if the car cannot be taken back because of an accident or breakdown). The following articles for personal use are also registered in the passport (although this is not checked very strictly when entering by charter flights; quite often, one need not declare anything): one camera, one film camera (both with an acceptable amount of film), one portable video camera (camcorder) with additional equipment and film, a pair of binoculars, a portable radio, a tape or a cassette recorder, a portable record player, a portable typewriter, a bicycle, sports and camping equipment (including inthis are surfboards and skies), a cartridge pistol and a hunting rifle with a maximum of 20 rounds of ammunition per person. If these articles are not taken back out of the country, they are subject to heavy import taxes. Other weapons, flowers, plants and walkie-talkies may not be taken into the country. For bringing in Greek and foreign currencies (→ *Money*).

When leaving the country, there are no restrictions on goods up to total value of £260 ($487). No antiques or artifacts whatsoever, be it only some shards of broken earthenware found in some excavation may be taken beyond Greek borders. Being caught in such an attempt will invariably bring the tourist behind bars; the Greeks have lost too many of their ancient artifacts this way.

For reentering the United Kingdom the normal European Union regulations apply.

Díkeos (Mt. Díkeos)

Reaching an altitude of 846 metres (2,766 feet), the Díkeos is the highest mountain on the otherwise relatively flat island of Kos. The mountain range is characterised by dense vegetation and perpetually filled springs — even in summer, there is always a pleasant breeze. It is especially the northern slope which has a very favourable climate. It is here that the most beautiful villages on the island are situated amid the lush green vegetation and these have conserved much of the natural simplicity once possessed by all villages on the island.

It is possible to climb the peak of the Díkeos from one of these villages called → *Zía*. However, it is not an easy hike and is better undertaken with an experienced local guide. Even in the middle of summer, the weather is very unpredictable here and can change quickly, causing critical situations for unexperienced hikers.

The small Chrístos Díkeos Church awaits all those who managed the climb to the summit.

Discounts

The holders of international student identification are granted a discount of up to 50% on normal admission to museums and archeological sites on Kos. Under some circumstances, some Greek airlines also offer reduced fares on domestic flights — information can be obtained in the → *Olympic Airways* office on Kos.

Economy

On Kos, as in other areas of Greece, *tourism* has become the most important branch of the economy.

The residents of Kos, who are anything but poor due to the favourable location, geography and climate of the island, have attained a standard of living which can well compete with other western industrialised countries. After tourism, *agriculture* is the island's second largest branch of the economy. Mostly olives and citrus fruits are cultivated on the island for export markets.

Owing to the favourable climatic conditions and the fertile soil, some fruits can even be harvested twice a year (especially the fast-ripening field fruits).

Fishing has never played an important role on Kos and even today, one will see only very few fishing boats here. The largest proportion of the fish served in restaurants has to be imported, especially since this part of the Mediterranean has almost no fish due to the extreme overfishing of these waters.

Quite a few small *handicraft shops* are kept in business by tourism, some of which could even register an increase in sales during recent years. Among these are potters, tailors, and weavers. Their production is almost exclusively to meet tourist demand.

There is no heavy industry on Kos — the island is orientated completely towards agriculture. Therefore, all consumer goods and many articles for everyday use must be imported.

Electricity

The voltage everywhere on the island is 220 volts. Although most places have quite modern standards, old sockets can sometimes be encountered; therefore, an adapter may prove helpful.

Eleón

Eleón is a hamlet without any importance whatsoever, located above the likewise rather uninteresting → *Tolári*, which can be reached by a road in quite poor condition. The view from here to the coastline of Tolári and Kardámaena is quite beautiful.

Embassies

Australian Embassy
37 D Souston St.
Athens, Greece
Tel: 644 73 03
open Monday to Friday 9 am to 1 pm

British Embassy
1 Ploutarchou St. at Ypsilantou St.
Athens, Greece
Tel: 723 61 11
open Monday to Friday 8 am to 1:30 pm

Canadian Embassy
4 Ioannou Genadiou St.
Athens, Greece
Tel: 723 95 11
open Monday to Friday 8:30 am to 1 pm

New Zealand Embassy
15-17 An. Tsoha St.
Athens, Greece
Tel: 641 03 11
open Monday to Friday 9 am to 1 pm

United States Embassy
91 Vassilissis Sofias
Athens, Greece
Tel: 721 29 51 / 721 84 00
open Monday to Friday 8:30 am to 5 pm

Entertainment

The choice of well-known entertainment in the form of bars and discotheques is enormous on Kos. Every tourist has the opportunity to find

one which best suits his or her taste.
Most taverns offer live music with dances, though mostly arranged for tourists (→ *individual entries*).

Equipment

No special equipment is required for Kos and even most extensive hikes can be undertaken without any problems. However, it is recommended to bring along good walking shoes for this as well as long trousers, especially when hiking off of the main trails (→ *Clothing*).

Fuel

Considering the traffic on the island, the network of service stations is completely sufficient. Most stations sell international brands but the

Sometimes green and fertile, sometimes dry and barren —landscapes of the Dodecanese

octane is usually lower. Thus, it is recommended to fill the tank with super — this is even a requirement for rental cars. Prices of normal fuel and super are more or less the same as in other western European countries. Diesel fuel is relatively inexpensive, costing around 25p (47¢) per litre. Since 1990, lead-free fuel is also available in Greece, costing around 50p (93¢) for one litre.

Geography

With an area of 290 square kilometres (about 180 square miles), Kos is the third largest island in the Dodecanese after Rhodes and Kárpathos. It is around 40 kilometres (25 miles) long and its width ranges from 2 to 10 kilometres (1¼ to 6¼ miles). The eastern end of the island, where Kos City is located, is only 3 nautical miles from the coast of Asia Minor. Long and flat, the island extends from east to west interrupted only by the Díkeos mountains rising up to 846 metres (2,766 feet).

The Bay of Kéfalos, which cuts into the island in the west narrowing it to a width of only 2 kilometres (1¼ miles) is simultaneously the island's only larger bay. Apart from this, the coastline runs completely straight and without any larger or smaller bays — quite atypical for a Greek island.

This is also the reason why Kos City, situated at the easternmost tip of the island, possesses the only harbour of the island which is worth mentioning and which is also large enough to accommodate larger ferries.

Broad plains extending across a tuff plateau cover the largest portion of the island, highly characteristic of Kos' landscapes.

The slopes of the Díkeos, especially in the north, have abundant water since the mountains trap the rainclouds. The vegetation is amazingly green.

Although the landscapes of Kos do not offer great variety, they are very suitable for extensive hikes and cycling because the countryside is flat. Olive trees typify the vegetation on the coastal plains, small forests on the slopes of the → *Díkeos* and numerous phrygána *(→ Vegetation)* grow in the island's interior.

Despite its straight coastline, the island does have numerous beautiful sandy beaches.

ΓΡΑΦΙΚΕΣ ΤΕΧΝΕΣ ΧΑΡ. Ι. ΠΑΠΑΔΟΠΟΥΛΟΣ Α.Ε.

Άγαλμα Ιπποκράτη (λεπτομέρεια), Ελληνιστικών χρόνων.
Statue of Hippocrates (detail). Hellenistic period.

ΚΩΣ
ΚOS

384762

ΚΩΣ

ENTRANCE
TICKET
ΔΡΧ.
DRS. **400**

Greetings

Just as at home, it should actually go without saying: when passing a village as a stranger or meeting a local resident one should greet them even without any knowledge of the Greek language. A friendly smile, a small nod can already be perceived as greeting and will usually be reciprodated. A greeting in Greek will certainly be rewarded with a benevolent and friendly smile. Even with a very limited command of Greek, it is possible to get through the day. Saying "Kaliméra" (good morning) is the right greeting untill around noon; "Kalispéra" (good evening) is already used in the afternoon and throughout the evening hours. The day ends with "Kaliníchta" (good night) when going to bed or seeing somebody off.

Moreover, during the entire day it is possible to greet someone with "Jássu" or "Jássas" (hello). "Jássu" is used for individuals one knows a little better. "Jássas" is used for several persons or as a polite form when speaking with strangers.

Health Insurance

It is recommended to take out a supplemental travel health insurance policy for the duration of the trip (→ *Insurance*). Greek physicians will charge directly for treatment. Upon returning home, one must present invoices for medical treatment and medication to one's insurance company. It is also recommended to have this documentation translated or made out in the English language (→ *Medical Care, Pharmacies*).

Hippocrates

Hippocrates (460-377 BC) was born on Kos as the son of a physician. During his early years, he lead an unstable life and travelled throughout the entire world known at that time. Thanks to him, medicine of that time was given a scientific basis because he demanded an exact method of observing human nature. Precise descriptions of diseases and logical conclusions for treatment were intended to help the physicians of that time in distinguishing themselves from charlatans and quacks. This is how the famous "Hippocratic oath" came into existence according to which all actions of physician underlie strict moral norms. The oath has kept its validity up to present (though in an updated form). Therefore, it shall be mentioned here in its original form. It is striking how relevant many sections of the text are even today.

"1. I swear by Apollo, the physician, and Asclepius and Hygieia and Panakeia and all the gods and goddesses as witnesses that I will fulfil this oath and contract to the best of my abilities and conviction.

2. I will honour him who has thought me this art as my parents and share my substance with him, and relieve his necessities if required and treat his offspring as my brothers and teach them the art, if they shall wish to learn it, without fee or stipulation; and that by precept, lecture and every other mode of instruction, I will impart a knowledge of the art to my own sons, and those of my teachers, and to disciples bound by a stipulation and oath according to the law of medicine, but to none others.

3. I will follow the system of regimen which, according to my ability and judgment, I consider for the benefit of my patients, and abstain from whatever is deleterious and mischievous.

4. I will give no deadly medicine to any one if asked nor suggest any such counsel; and in a like manner, I will not give to a woman any pessary to produce abortion.

5. Purely and piously I will preserve my life and my art.

6. I will not cut, not even those suffering from stones, but leave this task to men who practice this art.

7. Into whatever houses I enter, I will go into them for the benefit of the sick, and abstain from every voluntary act of mischief and corruption; and, further from the seduction of females or males, of freemen and slaves.

8. Whatever in connection with my professional practice or not, in connection with it, I see or hear, in the life of men, which ought not to be spoken of abroad, I will not divulge, as reckoning that all should be kept secret.

9. If I fulfil this oath and do not break it, I shall proceed in my life and my art by gaining the respect of all people for all the time. If I should ever break it, so let the contrary overcome me."

History

The history of Kos is full of suffering and changes like the history of the other Dodecanese islands.

Findings in the Aspri Pétra cave in the western portions of the island and on Mount Ziní prove that Kos was already settled during the neolithic period. There were also Mycenaean graves dating back to the period between 1500 and 1200 BC discovered so that one can conclude that the island was populated by the Achaeans near the end of the 14th century BC, bringing Kos under the influence of the Mycenaean culture brought by the Achaeans, who came from the Peleponnese and dominating the entire Aegean Sea. Around the same time inhabitants of Crete founded a trading post at what is now called Kos City. However, as on Rhodes, the Achaeans were the founders of the first settlement with real significance on the island, Astipálaia near Kéfalos.

Numerous mosques and minarettes are witness today of the former Turkish rule on Kos

The culture brought along by the Achaeans shaped Kos significantly. Between the 11th and the 9th centuries BC, the Dorians appeared on the island, allegedly led by the son of the mythical hero Hercules. Only after the Dorian colonisation does the island's history becomes more comprehensible and precise.

Together with Halikarnassós and Knídos in Asia Minor and the city states on Rhodes (Líndos, Ialyssos, Kamíros), the inhabitants of Kos united around 700 BC to the Dorian League of Six Cities (Hexápolis).

Under Dorian rule, the island developed an independent art and culture and the inhabitants were widely respected.

Around the same time, the inhabitants of Epidaurus (Peloponnesus) must have brought the Asclepius cult (→ *Asclepius Sanctuary*) for the first time to the island. However, the Dorian epoch on the island lasted only a relatively short time and as early as in 546 BC, the island fell under Persian rule. Here, it had to immediately participate in the battle of Salamís on the side of Persia with five ships.

In 477 BC, after the conclusive defeat of Persia, the island joined the Attica-Delos nautical federation and — after confused times with several changes of power — fought on the side of Athens in the Peloponnesian War from 431-404 BC; however, did not get involved in the domestic war between Athens and Sparta. Simultaneously, Greece flourished which also had its effects on Kos. However, domestic wars shook the island as well, causing unrest on Kos which almost led to a civil war. A party in favour of democracy and a party in favour of oligarchy (rule of several smaller groups) had formed on the island. The quarrels only ended when the two parties agreed to build a new capital on the eastern tip of the island — the site where Kos City is situated today. It was then connected to the other villages on the island. This took place in 412 BC and the new capital, which was actually built in 366 BC, quickly gained in importance as one of the largest commercial centres in the Aegean Sea. Splendid buildings and lovely streets ornamented the new city; on the outskirts, the great place of worship, the Asclepius Sanctuary was built simultaneously. This sanctuary (→ *Asclepius Sanctuary*) and the medical schools of → *Hippocrates,* who was born on Kos in 460 BC, attracted physicians and doctors from the entire antique world. After the death of

Alexander the Great who had conquered the island in 336 BC, it passed to the Ptolemies in 323 BC and taken over by the Romans in 130 BC as with the rest of Greece.

Since the Romans also appreciated Kos as an island for recreation, the reputation of the Asclepius Sanctuary quickly spread across the antique world and granted Kos an extremely affluent epoch. Most findings in the archeological museum in → *Kos City* are from this period. The island enjoyed several privileges under the rule of the Roman Empire since almost every Roman commander or emperor had visited the island at least once (in terms of today they were the first tourists).

Medical care was first-rate and, moreover, the Koseans started raising silkworms — the silk industry flourished and stimulated trade.

Even the Apostle Paul visited the island during his travels and introduced the Koseans to Christianity. In 431 AD, Kos even became a bishopric. Through the division of the Roman Empire in 395 AD, the island became part of the Eastern Roman Empire to be administered in subsequent years by Samos.

After the capital had been destroyed by an earthquake in 554 AD, it was abandoned by most of its inhabitants who fled the island. Little took place on Kos during the 700 years to follow.

In 1204, Kos was conquered by crusaders and consequently fell under the rule of Venice; exactly 100 years later, it was ruled by Genoa.

In 1315, Genoa suceeded rule of the island to the Knights of St. John, who developed Kos into an outpost to defend against the Turks and constructed several forts. Despite these efforts, the island was conquered by the Turks in 1523 and remained under their rule for 400 years. The Turkish occupying forces also liked the island and settled there. Even today, there are many Islamic Greeks on Kos who are decedents of the Turks who remained on the island after the Italians ousted the Turkish population. Today, they are Greek citizens and completely integrated into society.

It was only in 1912 that the Italians would free the island from the Turks and stay themselves as occupying forces.

In 1943, German troopss occupied the island to be followed by British troops at the end of the war. The British finally gave Kos, like all other islands in the Dodecanese, back to Greece.

This would mark the end of the varied and turbulent history of the island to date.

Holidays and Celebrations

Every day of the orthodox ecclesiastical year is dedicated to at least one saint. On each of these days every Greek person named after the respective saint will celebrate his or her saint's day which has about the same importance in Greece as a birthday would have elsewhere. Moreover, all villages celebrate the day of their special patron saint or of a saint after which the local chapel was named. Therefore, these holidays are only of regional importance, whereas the following is a list of the national holidays and celebrations.

Since almost all holidays and celebrations are derived from a religious background (except for legal holidays), the churches also have an decided influence in the way they are celebrated.

Apart from numerous religious holidays, there are some secular holidays rooted in Greece's history (all holidays marked with a * are only celebrated on Kos).

January 1, Protochroniá (New Year's Day). New Year's Eve in Greece is the night of Ai Vassílis who has the role of Father Christmas and brings presents. The night is celebrated within the family, playing cards or other games. Around midnight, the New Year's cake which contains a coin is cut. The one who has the piece with the coin will have good luck during the entire year to come.

January 6, Agía Theophánia. Mostly in coastal regions masses are held in honour of Christ's baptism. The highlight is when the priest throws the cross into the ocean and young men dive in to rescue it. (However, to guarantee the rescue the cross, it is meanwhile tied to a nylon line!)

March 25, the Annunciation celebration and simultaneously a historical holiday. March 25,1821 was the day when the uprise began against the foreign Turkish rule and occupation which lasted for centuries.

Easter begins with the Holy Week (Megáli Evdomáda) on Palm Sunday. It is the most important holiday for the Greek Orthodox Church and certainly constitutes a great experience for anyone who is able to take part in it. During the Holy Week, churches and house doors are decorated

with branches and woven palm leaves. On Good Friday, the burial of Jesus Christ is commemorated almost everywhere with solemn processions. The mass held on the eve of Easter Sunday has its climax around midnight with the priest proclaiming: "Christ is risen." And the congregation answers: "He is risen indeed." ("Christós anésti" - "Alithós anésti.") After the mass the Lent season is complete and during that very night people will come gather to eat the paschal lamb.
* April 23, Agios Geórgios in Pylí and in many of the small churches dedicated to St. George on the island.
May 1, is likewise celebrated with excursions and picnics. Doors are decorated with flowers and garlands.
June 24, here like in many other central and northern European countries midsummer is celebrated with bonfires.
* July 29, day of Agíi Apostóli in Andimáchia.

"Christ is risen" — this proclamation by the Orthodox Papa is the climax of Easter mass year after year

August 15, Mary's Ascension. Although this holiday is celebrated throughout Kos, the Panagía in Kardámaena is especially worth mentioning.

October 28, the so-called "Ochi-Day". It is celebrated in remembrance of the Greek government's "no" to Mussolini's ultimatum to surrender in 1940. Officially, this is Greece's national holiday.

November 21, Panagía in Ziá.

* December 6, Agios Nikólaos in Kos City. Although Christmas and Easter are very important religious holidays, presents are exchanged on New Year's Eve.

December 24 is not celebrated very much. Children walk through the neighbourhood singing the "Kálanda" (songs announcing the birth of Christ) together with good wishes and they receive small gifts.

The actual family holiday is December 25. Even in Greece, the Christmas tree has gained ground, although most are plastic.

One should keep in mind that all holidays may differ greatly in the way they are celebrated in different regions. Furthermore, there are some festivals that are only celebrated on Kos' small neighbouring islands (→ *individual entries*).

Hospitals → *Medical Care*

Icons

It is simply unimaginable that there would be a church or chapel in all of Greece or on Kos without an icon.

These images of worship are always recurrent in the founding legends of churches and monasteries, similar to visions of Mary in the Catholic Church. It was on account of the icons that small chapels and monasteries were erected in many places on Kos. Nevertheless, each icon has a history all its own.

For the Orthodox Christians, the icons are consecrated and holy. Prayers are spoken before the icons while crossing oneself; expressions range from mourning to joy, when even money is brought as an offering. There are quite a few icons said to have a very special miraculous powers.

On the one hand, icons are sacred; on the other hand, they are very close to the people. In processions, they are carried through the village streets.

Especially around Easter, the highest holiday for the Greek Orthodox Church, they are sometimes lent to other churches or even brought to other islands by ship.

The arrival of an icon marks the beginning of a festival in the village with dancing and celebrations where every resident wants to carry the icon even if only for a moment. If the year has been especially successful for the village residents, the icon is given money or other highly personal belongings.

In former times, the icons were usually painted with natural colours on wood and covered in slilver or sometimes even gold leaf.

Painting techniques and styles are mostly set, the themes are determined by tradition so that there are very few noticable deviations over the centuries. Thus, icons from different centuries are so similar that it is difficult to spot differentiating characteristics.

Every icon contains a certain theological statement with many aspects. However, icons for an Orthodox Christian do not have the same meaning as, for example, a religious painting might have for a Catholic. They are much more important. In Greek churches and monasteries, the icon is always a component of the so-call iconostasis, which is usually an extraordinarily richly embellished partition that separates the nave from the altar room.

Sometimes, the icons are part of the iconostasis, sometimes they are installed on the floor in front of it or placed on a table when space is limited.

Due to their age and the valuable materials used in producing them, the icons are exceptional treasures. Thus, some of the icons in churches and monasteries are priceless.

The icons are also the reason why all of Kos' churches are locked: unfortunately, visitors to the formerly open churches took advantage of the opportunity to take the icons or part of the iconostasis as souvenirs.

Insurance

It is recommended to take out a baggage insurance *(→ Crime)*. While travelling by car it is recommended to take out coverage for breakdown services with an automobile club or at least comprehensive insurance for the full duration of the trip.

Supplementary health insurance coverage will prove a wise decision since doctors expect payment upon treatment (→ *Medical Care*).

Kafenío(n)

The Kafenío is an important piece of social life in Greece. Actually, it is almost a social institution. No Greek village is complete and intact without the Kafenío. Even in times of rapid social change — even in Greece — the intitution of the Kafenío is hardly undergoing any changes. The clientele in a Kafenío still consists of men only. This is the place where Távli is played, heated discussions are carried out, village gossip is passed on — sometimes they are simply used to pass the time.

Usually one will not meet women here. If so, they are usually foreigners. Especially in small villages and on some remote islands, the Kafenío also serves as the only store and the only post office of the town. Here, the necessities of daily life can be bought. In some places that have not been so drastically engulfed by the wave of tourism, it is possible to spend hours on end in a Kafenío without even having to order something. However, this is not the case on Kos. Entering a Kafenío for the first time, one will probably surprised about the extremely sparse furnishings and uncomfortable interior. Bare walls, neon light — the atmosphere resembles more a waiting room at the station than a cozy meeting point. But after a while, one will be caught up in the atmosphere that a place like this radiates, wishing that this everyday Greek institution will linger as long as possible and not be displaced by lifeless bars with a cool artificial interior which, unfortunately, increasingly dominate the picture on Kos.

Kálymnos (excursion)

The island of Kálymnos is famous for its sponge divers and remains the last Dodecanese island to maintain a fleet of around 100 boats that set out every year in April.

However, the times that the residents of the island could make a living on sponge fishing are long since past which gave way to the establishment of tourism here as well. Kálymnos with its capital city Póthia is one of the very few islands that is not completely deserted in winter. Póthia is a lively city with a size no one would expect of such a small island.

Kálymnos is a rather mountainous island, generally very barren and dry, which allows agricultural cultivation in only very few valleys, the most famous of which is certainly the lush green Váthys Valley.

With Kálymnos, the visitor is presented with a piece of the genuine Greece — with no ornaments or cliches — and it is probably just this that makes the island is so charming.

The island is actually much too good for just a day-trip from Kos. It would be much better to take the time to explore the island to its full potential.

Accommodation / Transportation: Accommodation options are sufficient and connections between Kos and Kálymnos are very good.

Kálymnos / **Póthia**

With a population around 11,000, **Póthia** is one of the largest towns in the Dodecanese — and certainly one of the most Greek in character. Tourism certainly does not play such an important role as in other places; it is tolerated, sometimes welcomed, but the residents can do without it and without the problems tourism brings.

The main town of Kálymnos is a very colourful city, the houses shimmering in all imaginable pastel hues. Along the harbour boulevard, one can still see the old buildings from Italian colonial times. There are no skyscrapers at all. Póthia is a rather young city, first to be founded in 1850 by the inhabitants of Chóra, a city built above the Póthia after the fear of pirate attacks became a thing of the past.

Even today, sponges are sold along the harbour promenade — about 100 years ago, several Dodecanese islands made their living from this trade.

It is very nice to stroll through the city and watch the goings-on. The *Christ Church* on the Platía Eleftherías and the town's small museum, containing archaeological finds from the entire island are certainly worth seeing.

Kálymnos / **Excursions on the Island**

The city of **Chóra** around 4 kilometres (2 miles) from Póthia was founded much earlier. Today, however, both cities have grown together into one entity. Póthia's profile is dominated by the ruins of a *fortress* built by the Knights of St. John of Jerusalem on the ruins of the old Byzantine fortress. Unfortunately, the fortress has meanwhile almost completely fallen to ruins.

Above Póthia to the northwest is another *Kástro* or fortress, the "Kástro tis Chrissocheriás", named after the icon of the church, hidden by the massive walls.

At the base of Kastro hill, three old *windmills* are reminiscent of times gone by — perhaps maybe they will be restored one day.

Northeast of Póthia, one will find the *Eptá Parthéon Grotto* which was already a place of worship during antiquity. Numerous sacred artifacts have been found in this grotto so far.

On the way from Chóra to **Pánormos**, a small town on the western coast of the island, one will find what is probably the most important church on Kálymnos, the *Christós tis Ierusalím Church.*

Its foundation is said to go back as far as the 6th century. One can see that antique building materials among others were used in its construction. In addition, it was erected on the site of an antique shrine dedicated to Apollo. Inside the church, one will find a very beautiful mosaic floors.

In the **Dámos** region near Chóra, a cemetery from Hellenistic times and remnants of houses and city walls have been discovered. West of Póthia, one will have the opportunity to visit several monasteries which are still functioning, some of them even offer accommodation. Near the village of **Vothíni**, a very nice and quiet little mountain village, one can find the two most important monasteries: the *All Saints' Monastery* and the *Ekaterínis Monastery.*

The famous green *Váthys Valley,* the islands' most important region for agricultural production, is situated in the east. Here, one will see thousands of tangerine trees the, fruits of which are even exported.

Váthys is a small town with a harbour that is even smaller, without any tourism worth mentioning. So here one will quickly be integrated into the circle of local residents. Unfortunately, Váthys has no beach.

Starting in Váthys by boat, one can easily reach the *Daskalió coastal cave* with fascinating stalactits and stalagmites. Moreover, during the Turkish occupation, this was the place where a secret Greek school was hidden. The most important beaches and seaside resorts of Kálymnos are situated on the western coast near the small island of **Télendos**. This is the touristic focal point of Kálymnos and therefore the place where most hotels are located. **Mirtiés** is the region's most important town with a very interesting location on the strait of Télendos; the surroundings are astonishingly green.

However, beautiful sand and gravel beaches with all the necessary tourist facilities can also be found to the north near **Masoúri** and to the south near **Kandoúi.**

The island's northern extremeties are only sparsely populated, making it easy to find secluded beaches everywhere in this region. Moreover, the region is highly recommended for longer hikes through the lonely landscapes.

Kálymnos / **Practical Information**

Accommodation

In Póthia: C-category: "Evánik", Tel: 02 43/2 20 57, Od. Patriárchou Maxímou, double rooms priced around £12 ($22).

"Olympic", Tel: 02 43/2 88 01-3, Od. Agóu Nikoláou, double rooms prided around £12 ($22).

"Themelina", Tel: 02 43/2 26 82, beautiful old manor house, quietly situated, Od. Th. Kolokotronis.

D-category: "Alma", Tel: 02 43/2 89 69, Od. Patriárchou Maxímou, doubles priced around £10 ($19).

E-category: "Vazanéllis", Tel: 02 43/2 89 52, Od. Patriárchou Maxímou, double-room about £7 (12.50).

In addition, there are several private rooms, the more quiet ones are situated on the outskirts of town.

In Mirtiés: B-category: "Thémis", Tel: 02 43/4 72 30, doubles for around £13.50 ($25).

C-category: "Delfíni", Tel: 02 43/4 75 14, doubles priced around £10 ($19).

D-category: "Mirtiés", Tel: 02 43/4 75 12, doubles priced around £8.50 ($16).

E-category: "Paradise", Tel: 02 43/4 73 47, doubles priced around £7 ($12.50).

In Masoúri: B-category: "Arméos Beach", Tel: 02 43/4 74 88, doubles priced around £12 ($22).

C-category: "Aphrodíti", Tel: 02 43/4 74 20, doubles priced around £13.50 ($25)

"Masoúri Beach", Tel: 02 43/4 75 55, doubles priced around £13.50 ($25).

D-category: "Ioánna", Tel: 02 43/4 72 08, doubles priced around £7 ($12.50).

In both towns, there are also a limited number of private rooms available.

Banks: There are several banks in Póthia but most larger hotels and travel agencies will also exchange money.

Beaches and Swimming: There are almost no acceptable beaches near Póthia. The best beaches on the island are on the western coast which are easily accessible from Póthia.

Car Rental: There are several car rental agencies in Póthia, all situated near the harbour, but demand is very high in high season.

Medical Care: There is a sufficient number of English-speaking doctors in Póthia and even a small hospital.

Restaurants

The choice of restaurants in Póthia is abundant; here, only a few:

The "Zorbas" Tavern at Platía Martióu 25, good fish dishes, frequented by many locals.

The "Uncle Petros" Tavern, said to be the best tavern in town for fish is situated at the end of the harbour boulevard.

In the old part of the town one can find the tavern "Ksefteris", the oldest on the entire island — good Greek cuisine.

Near the customs office one will find the highly recommended tavern "Naftikos Omilos" with good food at reasonable prices. Apart from these there are several other good taverns — just try them out.

The tavern in Váthys situated directly at the harbour is also very beautiful.

The days when the residents of Kálymnos could live from sponge fishing are long since a thing of the past

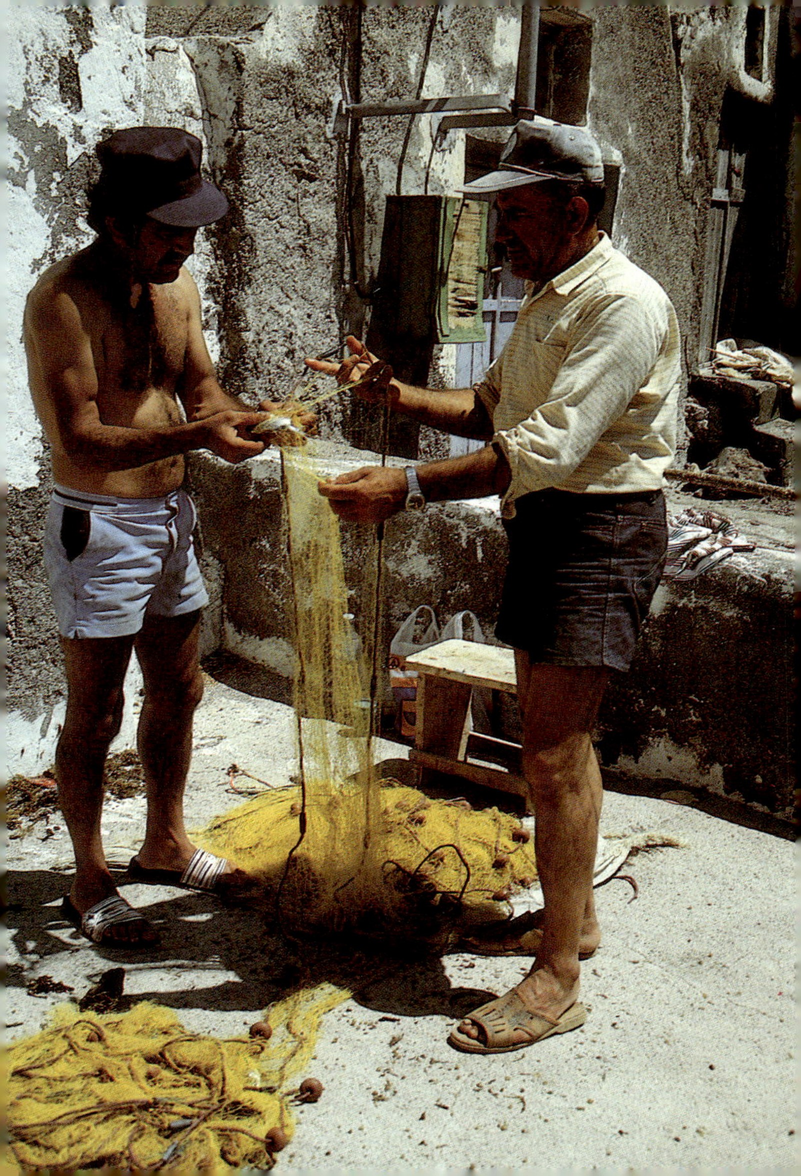

Shopping: Of course, sponges are the most popular souvenir from the island and they are still much more reasonably priced on Kálymnos than on the other islands or at home. The bigger a sponge, the higher the price (→ *Sponges*).

Stefanos Bablas' handcarved model ships are very beautiful. His small shop is situated in the middle of Póthia near Platía Kyprou.

Transportation

Buses: There are buses operating several times a day between the resorts on the western coast and Póthia. Bus fare is around 60p ($1) and 70p ($1.25). In addition, there is a bus operating daily to Váthys in the eastern portion of the island.

Ferries: The island can be reached daily from Kos; there are additional boats for day-trips. The duration of the voyage is around 1½ hours.

Air Travel: Near the village of Argos, a small airport is under construction but the exact date of completion has not yet been determined.

Taxis: The main means of transport on the island are taxis. These operate between Póthia and the resorts at more or less fixed fares.

Important Addresses: The tourist information office is behind the "Olympic" Hotel, open daily except Sundays, Tel: 02 43/2 93 10. Tourist police, directly along the harbour promenade.

Post Office: Od. Nik. Kalávrou (open: 7:30 am to 4 pm).

OTE: Od. Nik. Kalávrou (open: 7 am to 10 pm).

Olympic Airways Office: Od. Patr. Maxímou.

Taxi Stand: Platía Kyprou.

Kamári

Kamári is the name of the small harbour of Kéfalos situated on Kéfalos Bay — a town which is home to around 100 people and numerous taverns. It livens up in summer because of its location near one of the most beautiful pebble beaches on the island. Surfboards, pedal boats, and sunshades can be rented here (a chair and a sunshade cost around 70p/$1.25). The nearby beaches of "Camel", "Paradise", and "Mirva" are also very inviting.

Accommodation: There are numerous private rooms, some situated along the main road, making them less appropriate for a quiet holiday. The Kokalakis Hotel is an exception.
Transportation: The bus operating between Kos City and Kéfalos stops here as well.

Kardámaena

Kardámaena is situated 32 kilometres (20 miles) from Kos City and is the only settlement worth mentioning on Kos' southern coast except for Kéfalos, located only a few kilometres from the coastline. From here, one can enjoy the beautiful view of the island of Nísyros.

Normally, some 1,400 people live in Kardámaena but in summer this number increases enormously since the town is completely in the hands of package tour organisers who have transformed it into *the* tourist resort on the island. The reason for this must have been the sandy beach extending for several kilometres to both sides of town. Little is left of the former fishing village of Kardámaena; however, the touristic infrastructure is very good.

Meanwhile, one tavern follows the next, punctuated by discotheques, and new hotel buildings extend to both sides of town along the beach.

There are no sights worth mentioning. Kardámaena is best suited to all those who have high expectations in terms of beautiful beaches and a good touristic infrastructure.

Since the town is situated under the air traffic corridor of Kos' airport which is only 7 kilometres (4 miles) away, noise disturbances cannot be ruled out.

Kardámaena / **Practical Information**

Accommodation: The range of accommodation is very broad, hotels and guest houses in every category are available and there are even private rooms to rent (although only a limited number since the town is mainly geared to package tours). The following is only a small selection:
A-category: "Norida Beach", Tel: 02 42/9 12 31-2, doubles priced from £17 to £23.50 ($31.50 to $44).
B-category: "Alma", Tel: 02 42/9 13 65, doubles priced around £12 ($22).

C-category: "Panorama", Tel: 02 42/9 12 56-9, doubles priced around £12 ($22).
D-category: "Paralia", 25th Martiou 21, Tel: 02 42/5 12 05, doubles priced around £10 ($19).
"Milos", Tel: 02 42/9 14 13, doubles priced around £10 ($19).
During high season, one might have difficulties finding accommodation.
Banks: There is a bank at Kardámaena (open 8:30 am to 1:30 pm) but one can also exchange money at one of several travel agencies.
Beaches and Swimming: Kardámaena has the most beautiful beaches on the island, extending for several kilometres to the east and west of town. They are usually very sandy and slope gently into the water. The tide here is not as strong as on the northern coast and the beaches are well suited to children. In summer, however, they are usually very crowded, making it necessary to walk several kilometres to the west for

A worthwhile excursion destination: the island of Kálymnos with its attractive port city of Póthia

example, in order to find a secluded spot. Here, near Cape Chelóna, one will still find very nice bathing spots.

Car Rental: There are numerous car rental agencies which also rent out bicycles and mopeds. The differences in price are only marginal; one should make the choice according to the condition of the vehicle. The "Manos Rent-a-Car" near the OTE can be recommended.

Medical Care: There are several doctors and likewise several pharmacies in town. In difficult cases, one should consult a doctor at Kos City.

Restaurants: Unfortunately, no recommendations can be offered. In the centre of the town and along the beach boulevard are numerous taverns and bars that have for the most part adapted their cuisine to the tastes of tourists. The tavern "Ta Adelfia" is probably still the best bet because the value offered for the price is acceptable.

Shopping: There are no special tips. Most shops offer the same goods as in → *Kos City*.

Typical for Kos and all of Greece are the small windmills, some of which have been restored

Transportation: This town is connected with Kos City by a bus operating daily.

Important Addresses: The post office is in the centre of town (open 8:30 am to 8 pm). There is also an OTE office (open: 9 am to noon, 5 pm to 9 pm)

Kéfalos

Kéfalos is situated in the island's western extremities about 45 kilometres (28 miles) from Kos City and several kilometres away from Kéfalos Bay. Kéfalos has preserved much of its individuality and possesses a typical Greek atmosphere. With a population of about 2,000, it is the second largest town on the island after Kos City. Kéfalos is situated on a hilltop, thus offering a very beautiful view of the bay. For spending the night, however, the village of Kármari is much better suited.

Remnants of an ancient castle tower above the town and the ruins of → *Astipálea* the former capital of the island *(→ History)* are nearby. Kéfalos Bay is the best Kos can offer. A beach more than 2 kilometres (1¼ miles) long with very fine sand lines the beautiful shores of the bay. Although in high season, the bay is heavily frequented, it is not as crowded as for example the beach of Kardámaena. This is probably the reason why the Club Méditerranée (Tel: 02 42/7 13 11) has established itself on the bay's northeastern shores.

Starting from Kéfalos, one can hike to the abandoned monasteries *Agios Ioánnis Tchimianos* and *Agios Ioánnis Theológos* which are situated in complete solitude in the western portions of the island.

However, this peninsula is by far the most untouched part of Kos. Here one can find numerous small bays especially along the eastern coast, visited by only a handfull of people.

Kéfalos / **Practical Information**

In Kéfalos, one will find all the necessary facilities such as doctors, a post office, the OTE, and banks.

Accommodation (in Kamári): C-category "Kokalakis Hotel", Tel: 02 42/7 14 66, simple but nice rooms, small swimming pool, only bed and breakfast, doubles priced around £13.50 ($25).
D-category: "Sydney", Tel: 02 42/7 12 86, doubles around £12 ($22).
E-category: "Maria", Tel: 02 42/7 13 08, doubles from £5 to £7 ($9.50 to ($12.50).
In addition, there many private rooms available. Simply read the notices under "Rooms for Rent."
Cuisine: The speciality of this town are the famous thyme honey and the Kéfalos-Cheese which you should not miss to try. In → *Kámari,* the town's small harbour, are a number of taverns. The "Faros" is highly recommended for good value for the money. The taverns and Kafenía of Kéfalos itself offer even more atmosphere, where one can still experience a truly Greek ambience — a hectic chaos — somehow unique.
Transportation: There is a bus to Kos City operating daily.

Kos City

With a population of 11,000, Kos City is the largest city on the island and at the same time, the administrative capital of the Kos district.
Although the city has grown very quickly in recent years and is continually spreading out on both sides, it remains a rather charming city with an almost Oriental flair. The Oriental architecture and the numerous palms convey the felling that the visitor is right in the middle of Africa. Unlike Rhodes City, for example, there is no distinction between the old and new cities. Old mixes in harmony with the new which just might be what lends this city its special charm.
Everywhere, sidewalk cafés line both broad and narrow streets, even the relatively hectic traffic adds an almost cheerful touch.
Although in high season, Kos City is virtually invaded by legions of tourists, the town has successfully managed to protect its particular character from the influx of tourism.

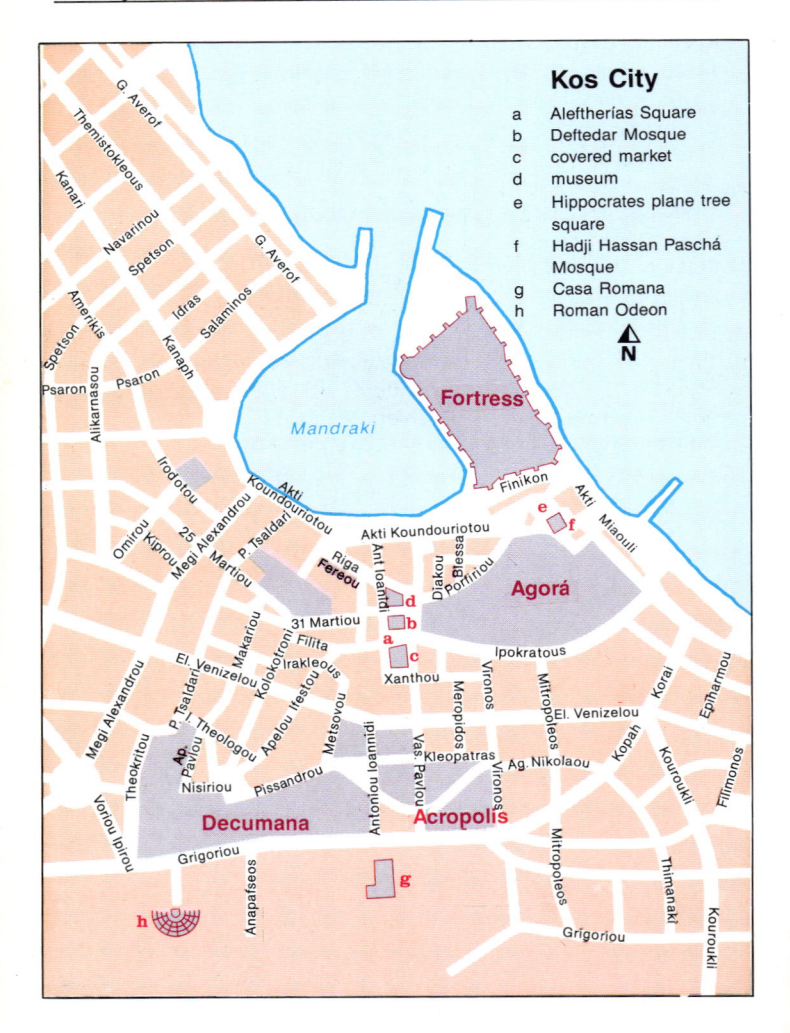

Kos City

- a Aleftherías Square
- b Deftedar Mosque
- c covered market
- d museum
- e Hippocrates plane tree square
- f Hadji Hassan Paschá Mosque
- g Casa Romana
- h Roman Odeon

Kos City / **History**

To a greater degree, the history of Kos City is the history of the island Kos *(→ History)*.

Far more remains to be seen of the ancient city today than from the mediaeval city. The reason for this is that the mediaeval part of town was almost completely destroyed by an earthquake in 1933.

Thus, only a few ruins remain from mediaeval buildings and those from the Turkish period. The city was then rebuilt by the Italians. Their buildings almost give an African impression. In addition, the earthquake opened up fantastic opportunities for the archaeologists to undertake large-scale excavations in the city. Visitors can see many of their finds (the excavations are not yet completed) in the museum *(→ Kos City / Sights)*. Thus, the earthquake brought destruction but also unearthed valuable testimonies of ancient times.

Kos City is like a living outdoor museum where the visitor meets up with remnants of its more than 2,300 years of history on every corner. The excavations are so impressive that one should take a couple of days to explore Kos City.

The city was founded around 366 BC by the Koseans *(→ History)*. This was at the same time when the city of Rhodes was founded. Kos City soon developed into the capital of the island and held this title until the 6th century AD.

It was then that a terrible earthquake must have destroyed the entire city for it is known that the entire population fled the city. It was left abandoned for 800 years.

Only the Knights of St John, who occupied the island, erected a new fortified knight's city on the site of the ancient Agorá (= market, town's centre). Many of the antique components of buildings where reused in construction then.

Thus continued the busy reconstruction of the city; however, when the Turks occupied the island, they also took possession of the city and continued construction in their own way. They consulted Greek architects and used antique marble when erecting the mosque of the city, for example. In 1933, a devastating earthquake once again destroyed the city, then to be reconstructed by the Italians. Excavations which began at that time, now offer the visitors a good impression of the structure of the ancient city.

After 1945, the modern part of the city developed and remained virtually unchanged up to present.

Kos City / **Sights**

There are abundant sights in Kos, the most important of these are certainly the various excavations within the city. For better orientation, have been subdivided into four main sectors.

The first sector comprises the region of the harbour with the ancient walls, the Agorá, the Basilica, and the Stoá (hall of columns). The second sector includes the eastern areas and the fortress as well as the ruins from the Byzantine era. This is where the archeological museum is located.

Sector three includes the western excavations, the thermal baths, the Odeon, the Casa Romana and the ancient temple square.

Finally, the forth sector comprises the central excavations with ruins from the Mycenaean epoch and the mosaic floors. All sectors are within walking distance of each other.

The central squares in Kos City are the Agorá followed immediately by Platía Eleftherías.

The ancient *Agorá* is located opposite of the harbour fortress and is the largest excavation site in the city in terms of area. Although visitors may only imagine how lively this marketplace first uncovered by the Italians in 1933 must have been in antiquity, they will certainly still be enthralled by the enchanting atmosphere it still possesses today. It is possible to walk around freely here; there is always the stub of a column to have a rest on and to watch the sunset without fearing that the site will be closed. One will discover clay vessels half buried, rendering the impression that it will take quite a while before the excavations are completed. Admission to the Agorá is free of charge.

To the east, an early Christian Church, the *Basilica of the Harbour* was built on an ancient Stoá.

The famous *Square of Hippocrates* is located to the north of the Agorá. The plane tree growing on it, the *plane tree of Hippocrates,* is said to be the oldest plane tree in all of Europe, planted in the 5th century BC.

Hippocrates is said to have taught his famous healing arts to his students in the shade of this tree (→ *Hippocrates, Ascepilus*). However, it may be doubted whether this tree is really that old but the Koseans go to great lengths to protect this tree; a tree which is indeed very old and which has a circumference of about 10 metres (33 feet). Several supportive and protective measures are intended to preserve and protect this tree for posterity.

The *Hadji Hassan Paschá Mosque* is situated next to this square. Built in 1786, it is delightful from an architectural perspective and has beautiful arched windows and external walls overgrown by numerous flowers. An arched bridge leads from the mosque to the *fortress complex* situated to the north. As on almost all of the Dodecanese islands, this fortress was erected by the Knights of St. John (this one in the year 1396) and served as defence post against the Turks. In former times, the fortress was also surrounded by a moat, but was later filled in. In 1522, the Knights of St. John gave up the fortress when it fell under the occupation of Sultan Suleiman the Magnificent, forcing the Knights' retreat from Rhodes and Kos.

Today, one can walk along the well-restored walls of the fortress. From here, one can enjoy the beautiful view over the rooftops to the city's harbour. The fortress is open daily except Mondays from 8:30 am to 3 pm. Admission costs around 85p ($1.80).

Although the fortress is not as impressive as its counterpart on Rhodes, a visit will certainly prove worthwhile. Stumps of columns, votive altars and numerous marble fragments of ancient Kos can be seen. Moreover, the view of the brilliant display of flowers on the walls is well worth the visit.

West of the Agorá at the central Platía Eleftherías, one will find the second mosque in Kos City, the *Deftedar Mosque* from 1725. It is also on this square where the city's relatively new *Archaeological Museum* is situated — a museum which should by all means be visited (open daily except Mondays from 8:30 am to 3 pm, admission is around 85p/$1.80). The museum is built the form of a Roman villa and displays sculptures from Hellenistic and Roman periods as well as findings from the → *Asclepius*

Excavations in the Southwestern Sector

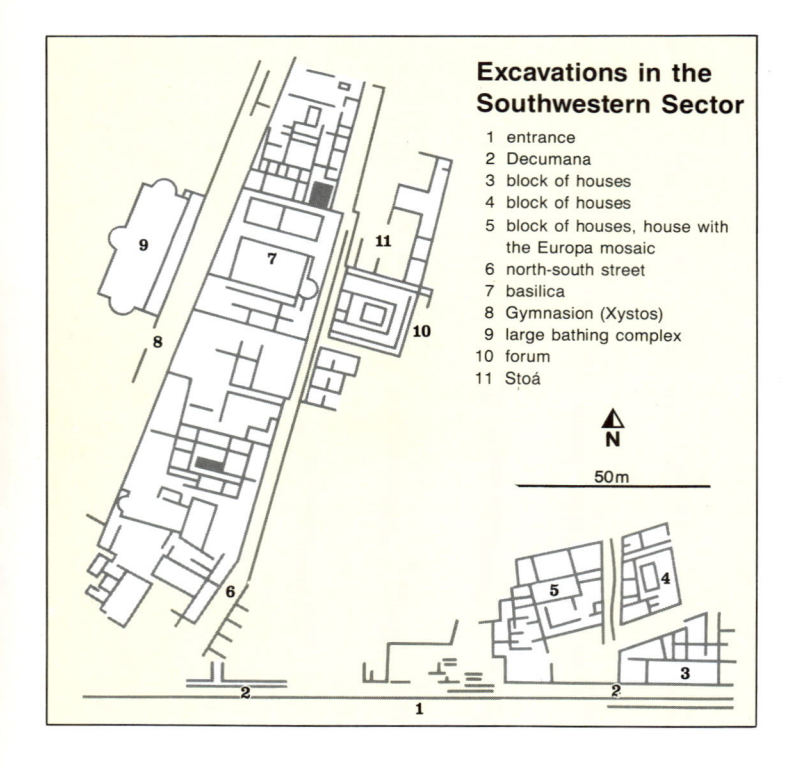

1. entrance
2. Decumana
3. block of houses
4. block of houses
5. block of houses, house with the Europa mosaic
6. north-south street
7. basilica
8. Gymnasion (Xystos)
9. large bathing complex
10. forum
11. Stoá

Sanctuary. The large *mosaic* in the inner courtyard of the building, depicting the arrival of Asclepius on Kos, is especially beautiful.

The third important excavation sector in the city is located to the southwest and was also first uncovered after the earthquake in 1933. These are the city's most attractive excavations. The *Casa Romana,* a restored Roman villa originates from the 3rd century AD and illustrates the way people lived in those times and the creature comforts and luxury the inhabitants enjoyed (if they could afford it). Open daily except Mondays from 8:30 am to 3 pm, admission around 85p ($1.80).

Also worth seeing is the *Odeon* which has been beautifully restored. Even today, concert and theatre performances take place here during the summer months — a truly fascinating backdrop for such events. Open daily except Mondays from 8:30 am to 3 pm.

The *Nymphaion* and the *Gymnasion* are probably the most dominating buildings of this excavation.

17 columns of the Gymnasion have been restored and rebuilt so far. In former times the columns provided a roof over the running track of the sports complex. The rows of columns originate from the 2nd century AD. The Nymphaion from the 3rd century AD was considered one of the most elegant and spacious building of that time. Marble columns surrounded the house in which the first public baths and toilets were located.

Located nearby, to the west of the city is the *House of Europa,* in which a magnificent mosaic floor depicts the myth of the kidnapping of Europa by Zeus in form of a bull. The walls are still partially covered with murals.

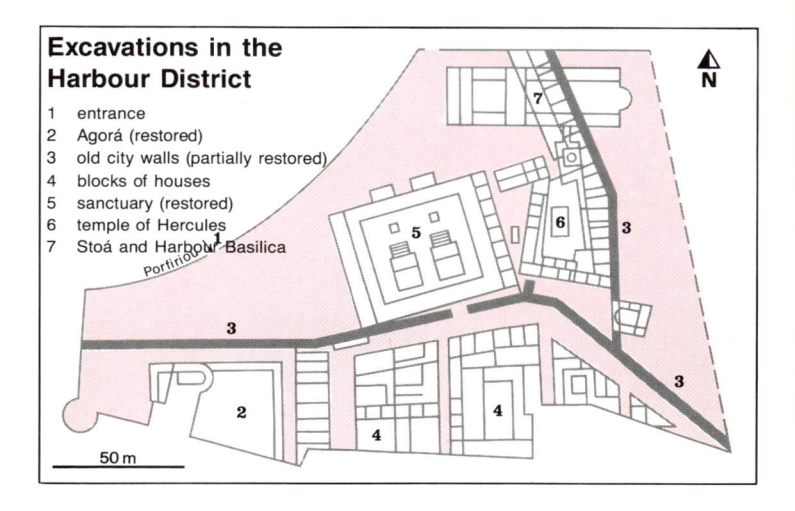

Excavations in the Harbour District

1 entrance
2 Agorá (restored)
3 old city walls (partially restored)
4 blocks of houses
5 sanctuary (restored)
6 temple of Hercules
7 Stoá and Harbour Basilica

Kos City 64

There are, however, other things to see in Kos than archeological sights. The entire city with its winding alleyways and its quaint little squares is just as much worth seeing. The small *Mandráki Harbour* (bearing the same name as its counterpart on Rhodes) counts among the particularities of the city. Here, yachts from all over the world drop anchor and the small excursion boats (→ *Excursions)* depart from here. This is the area where Kos City presents itself from its more international side; at the *Aktí Koundouriótou* which surrounds the harbour, one will find numerous elegant cafés. However one will have less the impression of being on a Greek island than in a chic Mediterranean town.

In Kos City, the modern merges with the ancient going hand in hand — probably the secret to Kos City's fascinating charm.

Kos City / **Practical Information**

Accommodation: Since in Kos City the new and the old part of the town with their entertainment districts merge into each other, it is not easy to find a quiet accommodation right in the city. Here are some suggestions:

A-category: "Dímitra-Beach", Tel: 02 42/2 85 81-2, doubles priced around £27 ($50).

B-category: "Georgia", Od. El. Venizélou 63, Tel: 02 42/2 85 77, doubles priced around £12 ($22).

"Kos", Od. Vassíleos Georgíou 31, Tel: 02 42/2 24 80-1, doubles priced around £17 ($32).

C-category: "Acropole", Od. Panagi Tsaldári 4, Tel: 02 42/2 22 44, doubles priced around £12 ($22).

"Ekaterini", Od. Panagi Tsaldári 8, Tel: 02 42/2 82 85, doubles priced around £15 ($28.50).

"Elma", Aktí Koundourióti 11, Tel: 02 42/2 29 20-1, doubles priced around £10 ($19).

"Kamelia", Od. Artemissías 3, Tel: 02 42/2 89 83, doubles priced around £12 ($22).

D-category: "Helena", Od. Megálou Alexándrou 5, Tel: 02 42/2 27 40, doubles priced around £10 ($19).

"Dodecanessus", Od. Alex. Ipsilántou 2, Tel: 02 42/2 84 60, doubles priced around £8.50 ($16).

E-category: "Alexis", Od. Irodotou 9, Tel: 02 42/2 87 98, doubles priced around £8.50 ($16).

"Fotis", Od. Porfiríou 21, Tel: 02 42/2 38 89, doubles priced around £10 ($19).

The tourist police and the EOT tourist information *(→ Kos City / Important Addresses)* will also help in locating private accommodation.

Tip: The only official camping area on the island is situated around 4 kilometres (2½ miles) east of the city on a coastal road. It is called "Kos Camping" (Tel: 02 42/2 39 10 or 2 32 75). The price per person and tent is around £2.50 ($4.50). The camping area is rather small with ample shade and clean sanitary facilities. There is a tavern and a motorcycle rental within the camping area. Moreover, the campsite is easily accessible by bus from Kos City *(→ Kos City / Transportation)*. There is no official youth hostel on Kos but the EOT *(→ Kos City / Important Addresses)* can provide addresses for very inexpensive guest houses with very simple accommodation and prices similar to youth hostels.

Banks: Most of the banks are located in the newer part of the city (at Od. El. Venizélou) and around the Mandráki Harbour (near the Aktí Koundouriótou). These are generally open only in the morning from 8:30 am to 1:30 pm, although some exchange counters are open in the afternoon, but this remains an exception to the rule. Apart from the normal business hours, many of the travel agencies will exchange money at the same rate (look for exchange rates posted in shop windows).

Beaches: To the east and west of the city, one will find extensive sandy beaches with all necessary facilities, although these are quite crowded. This is especially true for Merópis Beach east of the city. Also to the east of the city at a distance of 6 kilometres (4 miles) is Dímitra Beach with small bays, pebble and sand beaches and a similar number of visitors. Nor will one suffer from acute lonliness on Faros Beach west of Kos City. Those looking for a more quiet section of beach should go to the northern coast near → *Mastichári* (or to → *Kéfalos Bay)*. Buses operate regularly between these beaches *(→ Kos City / Transportation)*.

Bicycle Rental: Owing to the good streets and the rather flat topography of the island, cycling on Kos enjoys growing popularity. Correspondingly there are numerous rental agencies.

However, it is justified to be cautious when renting a bicycle because not all of the bicycles correspond to the safety standards one might be accustomed to. The price depends on the condition of the bicycle and is usually between £1 ($2) and £1.80 ($3) per day.

Car Rental: There are several Greek and international agencies in Kos City. The prices correspond to prices on other Greek islands. Here, some addresses:

Avis, P. Tsaldári 3, Tel: 02 42/2 42 72, and at the airport Tel: 02 42/5 14 55;

Budget, P. Plessa 2, Tel: 02 42/2 24 55;

National, Od. Ant. Ioannídi 3, Tel: 02 42/2 28 46 and Od. L. Virónos 10, Tel: 02 42/2 88 28;

Stamatis, Od. Nafkírou 1, Tel: 02 42/2 40 62;

Trust, Od. Eleft. Venizélou 30 A, Tel: 02 42/2 33 15.

Prices start around £23.50 ($44) per day, including mileage. Renting a motorcycle starts around £7 ($12.50) a day. When renting for several days, discounts can be negotiated (→ *Car Rental*).

Medical Care: Owing to its several thousand year-old tradition alone, medical care is of high standards in Kos City.

Hospital of Kos: "General Hippokretian Hospital", Od. Hippokrates 32, Tel: 02 42/2 23 00. This is an exceptionally modern and well-equipped hospital with a 24-hour emergecy service

There are also sufficient general practitioners in Kos City. A list of English-speaking doctors is available at the EOT tourist information office in Kos City or directly at the hospital. One general practitioner is, for example, Adonis Peides, Od. Hippokrátous 6, Tel: 02 42/2 43 84. There are also a sufficient number of pharmacies in the city.

Night Life and Entertainment: Kos City sets no limits on entertainment. Especially at the beaches near the city, but also in within the city, one will find numerous discotheques.

Bouzouki bars which local residents still enjoy visiting can be found at Od. Kanári (the "Aquarius") and to the west of the city at → *Lámbi Beach* (the "Vaghiera"). Here, live music is played often played until the wee

During a stroll through Kos City, one will repeatedly encounter interesting churches

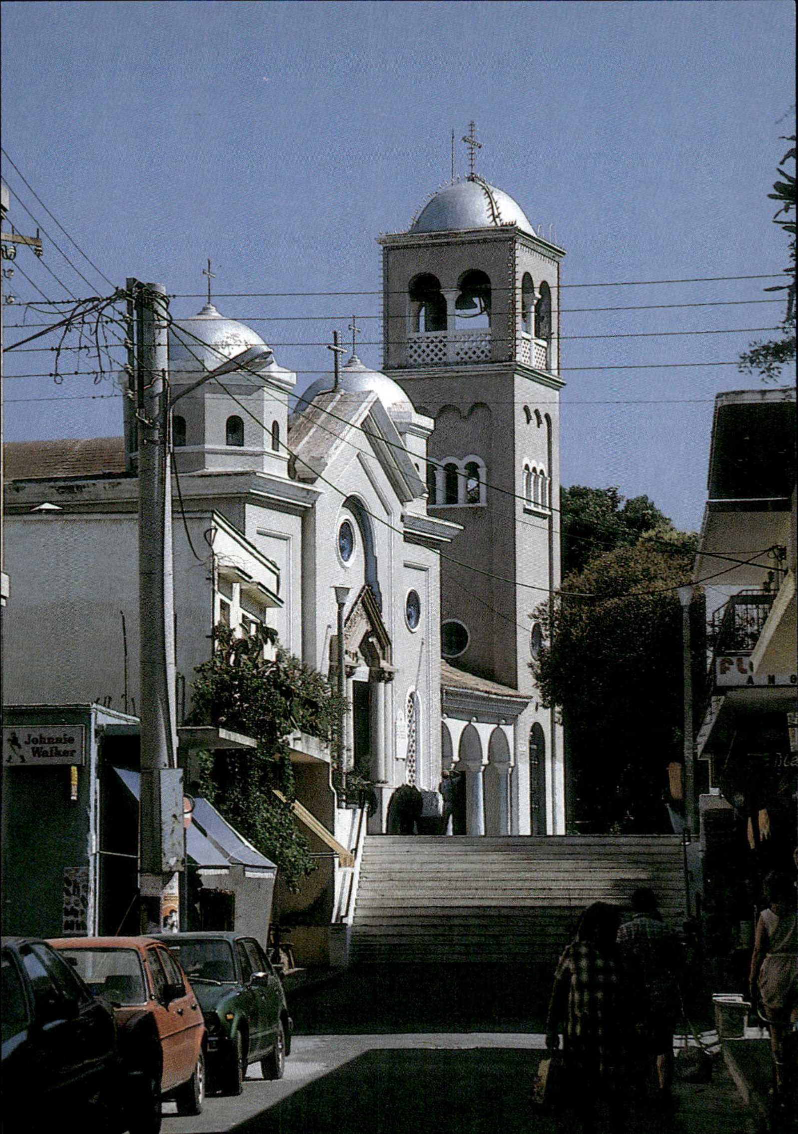
Johnnie
Walker

hours of the morning; however, these bars are quite expensive. But whenever the residents of Kos splurge on a Bouzouki evening, they never pay attention to money.

Restaurants: With regard to the restaurants of Kos City, a trend which is already apparent on many Greek islands can be observed on Kos as well: more quantity instead of quality, less food for more money, and more and more adaptation of the food to tourist preferences.

Thus, it is not too easy to provide recommendations. The most expensive restaurants are at the Aktí Koundourióti near Mandráki Harbour and around the Platía Eleftherías. Not exactly favourable in price, but a nice place to sit is the restaurant "Drossia" at the Od. Nafklírou north of the Agorá, serving good quality food. It is definitely worthwhile to pay a visit to the "Anatolia Hamam" Tavern on Od. Nisírou (Old Town). The tavern is housed in an ancient Turkish bath which makes for a rather different and unconventional atmosphere. Very good grilled dishes at reasonable prices. Address: Od. Nissírou, Tel: 02 42/2 33 35.

One of the restaurants which is still rather reasonable in price is the "Noufara" on Od. Kanári. Good grilled dishes are served here as well. Other recommendations include: the "Plátanos" Restaurant located directly at the Platía Hippokrátous. Guests are seated under a very old plane tree (→ *Kos City / Sights*) but it is quite expensive. Also worth recommending: "Limnos" Tavern situated directly along the harbour, good food and a wide selection.

East of the camping area, one will find the "Tassos" restaurant which is not exactly cheap but does offer food of excellent quality.

Very beautiful indeed, an authentic oúserie can be found at the El. Venizélou and is called "I oréa Kos" (beautiful Kos). Here, the ouzo is still served with small mezédes (snacks) as used to be customary in almost every oúserie. For the lighter appetite, one will meanwhile find hamburger and souvlaki stands on just about every corner — whether or not this is a necessity for Greece can be argued.

Shopping: Kos is a zone with special customs regulations, making it possible to purchase a number of articles at very favourable prices. This is especially true for tobacco and spirits. These are much less expensive than on the mainland and prices sometimes even lie below those in duty-free shops.

The best place to buy fruits and vegetables is the covered market with the oriental flavour at Platía Eleftherías. This interesting building with beautiful arcades is the scene for what may seem like Oriental bazaars every day. The streets Od. Hippokráous and Od. El. Venizélou begin at the Platía. Along with their side-streets, they constitute the main shopping areas for everything a tourist could desire. Between the Platía Eleftherías and the southwestern excavation sector is the so-called "Old Town" area, a maze of narrow alleyways and squares with only very limited traffic. It is here where most of the jewellery, fur and souvenir shops as well as countless cafés and restaurants can be found. The small Platía Diágora dominated by a minaret makes for a very romantic setting.

In addition, all sorts of souvenir-type articles can be found in Kos City, although much of it is tacky or mass-produced. On Od. Kolokotróni, however, one can find a ceramics shop with a very beautiful inner courtyard. Here, one will be able to find tasteful ceramics at reasonable prices (which does not necessarily mean cheap). At number 13, Od. Hippokátous, one will find the icon painter Katapodis' shop. Here, one can observe the process of painting an icon and buy one of these beautiful pieces of craftsmanship. These are not antiquities *(→ Customs Regulations)* but very charming and highly individual souvenirs. All icons are painted by hand and prices start around £34 ($63). These icons are very different from the other tacky icons available on the island.

Leather Goods are sometimes also relatively inexpensive but be sure to pay careful attention to the quality.

Good jewellery and furs are sometimes up to 30% less expensive, but bear in mind that good knowledge of jewellery is necessary. In addition, the goods must be declared when returning home *(→ Customs Regulations)*.

With regard to all articles, it is recommended to compare prices in various shops before showing definite interest. It helps in appearing more self-confident if one knows the appropriate price for an given article.

Transportation

Air Travel: Those prepared to spend a little more money can choose to use aeroplanes as their means of transportation. Kos' international airport is situated near the town of Andimáchia about 25 kilometres (15 miles) from Kos City. Especially during the summer months, charter planes from all over Europe land here. Moreover, → *Olympic Airways* offers good connections to the Greek mainland and the neighbouring islands. Buses operate from the Olympic Airways office in Kos City to every flight at the airport and vice versa. Bus fare to the airport is around 40p (75¢) (→ *Kos City / Important Addresses*).

At present, the following flights are in operation from Kos: to Athens — around £35 ($70), to Rhodes — around £23.50 ($44), to Léros — around £12 ($22), to Sámos — around £20 ($37.50), to Thessaloniki — around £69 ($129). In the near future, there will also be a scheduled flight to Kálymnos (as soon as the airport there is completed). More details can be obtained from the Olympic Airways office, Od. Vasílios Konstantínou 22, Tel: 02 42/2 83 31 in Kos City. Despite the large number of travellers, the airport on Kos is still rather primitive and is usually completely overrun in summer.

In addition, the buses from Andimáchia usually go through to the airport; despite this, one will probably not be able to avoid taking a taxi since the buses operate only sporadically.

Buses: Any place on Kos can be reached by bus; however, the bus schedules are more adapted to the needs of local residents than to those of the tourists. Therefore, buses often run from the villages to Kos City in the morning and return in the afternoon. Meanwhile, however, compromises between the different needs of the local residents and the tourists are being identified so that holiday-makers do not necessarily have to spend the night in a small village when actually wanting to visit Kos City.

The bus terminal is located some 500 metres from the harbour at Od. Ioannídi, near to the Olympic Airways office. Current schedules can be found at the bus stops or can be obtained from the EOT. Telephone information service: 02 42/2 22 92.

Bus fares are relatively high in relation to Greek incomes (e.g. Kos City — Kéfalos about £1.20/$2.20) which makes taking a taxi a viable option. At present, the following buses are in operation: twice daily to Asfendioú — around £4/$7.50; three times daily to Pylí — around £5/$9.50; three times daily to Andimáchia — around £8.50/$15.65; twice daily to Masti-

chári — around £6/$11.25; four times daily to Kardámaena — around £7.35/$13.75; and three times daily to Kéfalos — around £10/$19. Sometimes, the destinations often involve diversions so that smaller towns are also served by the bus system. The bus stop for municipal buses which connect the centre with the suburbs, is located in front of the city hall in Kos City. Fare for Kos City — Asclepius is around 35p/65¢.
Ferries: Kos offers excellent opportunities for taking excursions by boat. Being situated in the favourable central Dodecanese, there are ferries to almost all of the Dodecanese islands, the Greek mainland, the northern Aegean Islands and to the Cyclades. Although some of the ferry lines are not coordinated with each other and sometimes waiting periods of a day or two have to be expected, the overall service is very good with a wide selection of destinations.

Excursion boats, ferries and private yachts: the harbour of Kos City is always filled with activity

Kos City

Most shipping agencies are located at the Mandráki harbour. The EOT (→ *Kos City / Important Addresses*) has an overview of the current ferry connections including the addresses of the agencies.

Please note that the prices for excursion boats to the neighbouring islands are much higher than the regular ferry lines, and of course, most agencies are very interested in selling tickets for these excursion boats. If one does not manage to get a ticket for a particular line before departing on the trip, it is no problem to buy a ticket on board without a surcharge. Unlike the excursion boats, ships do not dock at Mandráki Harbour but at the huge mole near the fortress which is still under construction.

At present one can use the following ferries:

Destination Rhodes: direct by night ferry, operating daily. Duration of the trip: 4 hours. Departure time from Kos City: every night around 3 am. The names of the ferry boats are "Ialyssos", "Kamíros", "Alcéos" and "Omiros".

Kos — Rhodes on the Dodecanese Line: here, all islands between Kos and Rhodes are served. These are Nísyros, Tílos and Symi, entailing a total travel time of 8 hours. The line circulates two to three times a week.

Kos — Rhodes by express boat is offered at least once a day and takes only two hours.

Destination Piraeus: Kos — Piraeus by night ferry with stops at Kálymnos (about 1½ hours; from Mastichári only 50 minutes), Léros (2½ hours), and Pátmos (an additional 1½ hours). Total travel time: 14 hours, departure from Kos daily around 5 pm. Kos — Cyclades — Piraeus once a week, via Astipálea, Amorgós, Náxos and Páros. Duration of trip: over 20 hours.

Northern Dodecanese: Kos — Northern Dodecanese — Sámos, at least twice a week with the Dodecanese Line. Here, stops are also made at all the islands along the way such as Lípsi, Arkí and Agathoníssi. The duration of the voyage Kos — Pythagórion (Sámos) is around 12 hours.

Turkey: During the summer, there is an express hydrofoil to Rhodes once daily. The price is around £17 (31.50) for a one-way trip. Information is available from the Hydrofoil Office at the harbour. In particular, the large ferries to Piraeus and to Rhodes are very comfortable and clean. The "Kamíros" and the "Ialyssos" are especially worth mentioning.

Moreover, there are boats to → *Bodrum in* → *Turkey;* however, only for day trips.

Taxis: There are quite a few taxis on the island. The taxi stand in Kos City is located near the harbour at the fortress.

When making a cross-country trip by taxi, one should by all means negotiate the price in advance. Within the city, the price is measured by the taxometer (a price for orientation: the taxi ride from Kos Airport to Kos City costs around £6.70/$12.50); within the city, there is a minimum fee of 67p ($1.25). Taxi switchboard: 02 42/2 27 77.

Important Addresses: EOT tourist information, Aktí Koundourióti 9, Tel: 02 42/2 87 24

Tourist Police, Aktí Koundourióti 9, Tel: 02 42/2 85 07

Olympic Airways, Od. Vasílios Konstantínou 22, Tel: 02 42/2 83 31, at the airport Tel: 02 42/5 12 29

Post Office, Od. El. Venizélou 14, Tel: 02 42/2 22 50 (business hours: Monday to Friday 7:30 am to 2:30 pm, closed on weekends). It is recently said that the post office is also open on Saturday and Sunday mornings.

OTE, Od. L. Virónos 6, Tel: 02 42/2 24 99 (business hours: Monday to Friday 7:30 am to 10 pm).

Hospital, Od. Hippocrates 32, Tel: 02 42/2 23 00.

Agencies for ferries: most of them are situated on the Mandráki harbour.

D.E.A.S., municipal bus company, Aktí Koundouriótou, Tel: 02 42/2 82 23.

KTEL — cross country buses, Od. Kleopatras, Tel: 02 42/2 22 92.

Lámbi

Lámbi is the "home-beach" of Kos City, situated to the north making it also rather crowded during the summer. It is within easy walking distance from the city and is, therefore, frequented by numerous tourist. The nicer beaches can be found in the western portions of the island *(→ Beaches)*. Most hotels at Lámbi are booked by European travel organisations during the summer and the taverns here have already adapted to the eating and drinking habits of the visitors.

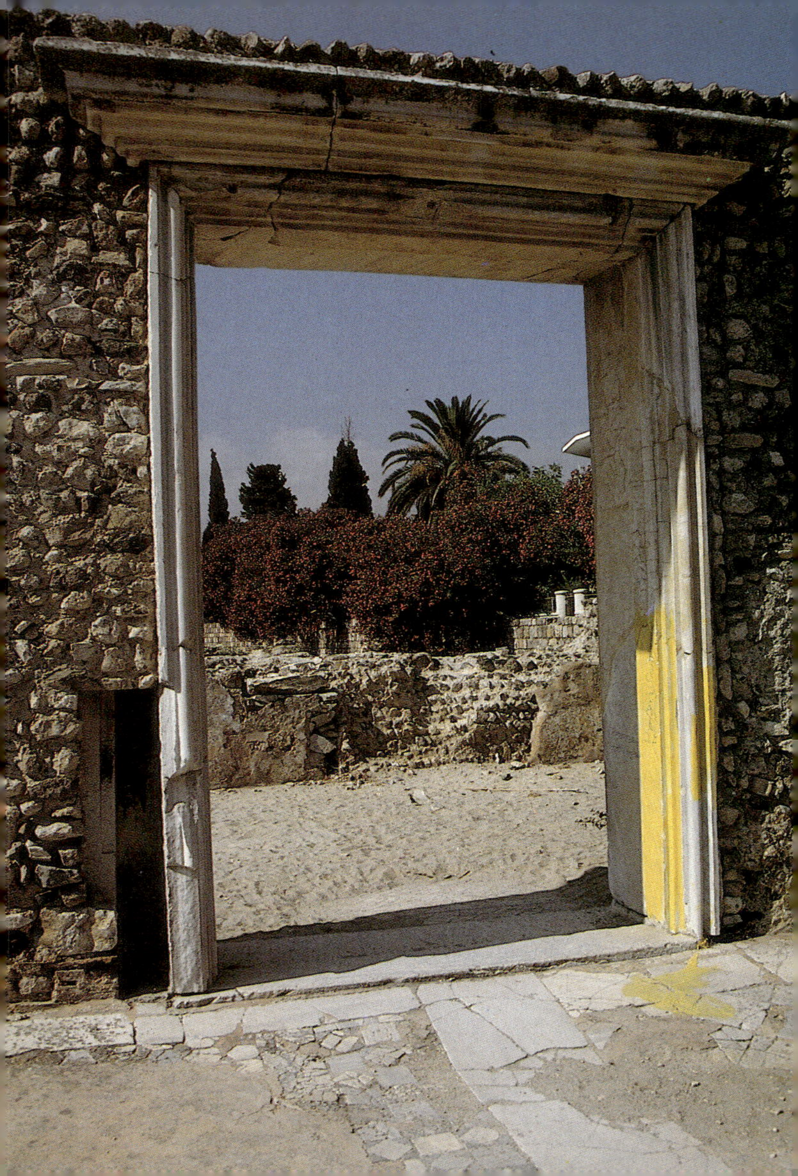

Language

The first difficulty a foreigner must usually overcome with regard to Greek language is the spelling, meaning the use of the Greek alphabet. However, quite a few the letters are quite familiar from mathematics and many of the capital letters resemble the Latin ones.

The second difficulty is pronunciation which is slightly different from English. For the less energetic, there is of course always the option to continue speaking English — there will always be someone who will at least understand; however, in order to make more personal contact, some basic knowledge of Greek language will prove very helpful. Since this is not a language guide, the Greek language will only be handled briefly in this guide. The most important thing is stressing the proper syllable (for this reason, all Greek words and names appearing in this book are marked with an accent on the stressed syllable). This is very important because even in short words consisting of only two syllables, the stress can completely change its meaning (for example, póte = when, poté = never.)

Unfortunately, the phonetic alphabet used here cannot bring across all the subtleties of Greek pronunciaton. As a rule, the alphabet used makes the attempt translate every Greek word the way it would be pronounced. Sometimes, however, it was necessary to deviate from the structure in order to make places, for example, recognisable. Some of the exceptions are for instance:

— if a "y" appears in the name of a place it is pronounced as "eh".
— "g" before "i" or "e" (as in Agía) is always pronounced as a "y".
— The "u" is spelled in Greek with "ou". This guide uses the "ou" only in names in order to facilitate the recognition effect. It is, however, pronounced as simple "uh".

Now some explanations of typical Greek sounds that cannot be translated into Latin spelling:

ch — generally as in "loch", but softer when followed by "e" or "i".
g — generally "g" as in "garden"; before "e", "i" like "y" as in "you" (e.g. Agía = Ahyíah).

Ancient sites on Kos are inevitably linked to Greek mythology

Language 76

a, e, i, o, u — always short and open, "a" as in "altar", "e" as in "pay", "i" as in "tin", "o" as in "optician", "u" as "ou" in "you".

Now some of the most important words:

yes	ne málista
no	óchi
please, thank you	parakaló, efcharistó
all right, good	endáxi, kalá
excuse me	signómi
that's okay	dhen pirási ("dh" like "th")
general greeting, hello and goodbye	jássas
how much is....	póso káni
this one (m, f, n)	avtós, -í, -ó
that's too expensive	íne polí akyriwó
I would like	thélo ("th" like "th")
I don't understand	dhen katálava
where is...	pu íne
a bank	mía trápesa
the post office	to tachidhromío
a physician	enas jatrós
the hospital	to nosokomío
the harbour	to limáni
the toilet	i tualétta
the airport	to aerodhrómio
what time is it?	ti óra íne
hotel	xenodhochío
restaurant	estiatório
tavern	tavérna
water	neró
wine, beer	brasí, bíra
bread, meat	psomí, kréas
fish, salat	psári, saláta

potatoes, rice	patátes, rísi
grapes, melons	stafília, karpúsi
coffee, tea, milk	kafés, tsái, gála
mineral water	sódha, metallikó neró

Tip: After having found the right word in the dictionary and even being able to pronounce it more or less correctly noting the accents, one might see nothing but baffled expressions. What might be wrong here? Probably one came across a word from "Katharevusa" an artificial standard language consisting of old and new Greek components. Although no normal person in Greece understands this language and it is no longer the official language, remnants can still be found frequently (for example, in dictionaries as mentioned above).

Léros *(Excursion)*

Léros is actually too far from Kos for just a day-trip. One-way on a large ferriy stopping at Kálymnos takes between 3 and 4 hours. However, it is of course *possible* to take only a day-trip. The island is very diverse and astonishingly green with a turbulent past. During the military dictatorship, it was here that the largest prison for political prisoners in Greece was located — a fact which is still a burden to Léros today. At the same time, Léros is home to one of the largest mental asylums in Greece, providing more than 1,000 of the local residents with jobs.
It is quite possible that these facts have prevented numerous tourists from visiting the island. When confronted with the untouched green landscape and the numerous small beaches carved deep into the rock and the beautiful sandy beaches with rolling hills in the background, there is hardly any other conceivable reason.

Léros / **Agía Marína**

Strictly speaking, Agía Marína consists of three settlements that have grown together. These are Agía Marína, Pantélí and Plátanos. The town

Léros (Excursion)

is situated slightly toward the eastern side of the island, more or less at its centre. Agía Marína is a place rich in typically Greek architecture: small white houses, classical patrician houses, small alleyways, and a *Venetian fortress* towering above the entire town. Although many new houses have been constructed in recent years, Agía Marína still preserve a lot of its original atmosphere.

The fortress was erected on the site of the ancient Acropolis. The fortress was important during the Byzantine epoch as well since it was the place where the saint Chistódoulos stayed. He was later to found the famous St. John's Monastery on → *Pátmos*. The fortress, which one can visit today, is still in the same condition as it was when built by the Knights of St. John.

The well-preserved walls and the *Panagástaou Kástrou Church* inside with an icon from 726 AD inside which is accredited with miraculous powers are worth seeing as is the beautiful view over vast parts of the island.

On the mountain opposite the fortress, one will see some *windmills* still in rather good condition. These could formerly be found on every island by the hundreds.

In addition, the small *municipal library* adjacent to the *Archaeological Museum* are worth a visit. Also be sure to see the *Agía Paraskeví Church* and the other beautifully restored classicistic buildings that were built by wealthy Greeks living abroad. They are constructed in an unique architectural style typical for Léros, combining classicistic elements with the island's traditional architecture.

In a number of respects, Agía Marína meets the expectations of a "typical Greek" island town. It is highly recommended to stay for a longer period on Léros.

Léros / **Lakkí**

Lakkí is the island's main port, situated in a deep bay on the western coast.

Lakkí is the strangest of all Greek harbour towns. To the arriving visitor, it does not seem Greek at all: the town seems lifeless and almost deserted, the broad avenues are lined with mighty classicistic buildings usually found in Italy and everything seems somehow exaggerated in proportion.

Lakkí was designed by the Italians as capital and administrational seat but was never accepted by the local population. They prefered to remain in Plátanos. When arriving by ship in the large natural bay carved deeply into the rocks, it is very easy to image the strategic importance of this location during World War II.

Léros / **Excursions on the Island**

Léros is a rather flat island so that exploring it on foot or by bicycle is easy.
The north is dry and barren; the south is the main area for agricultural production.

A cool breeze off the sea makes for a pleasantt climate even during the summer months

Léros (Excursion)

In the northern part of the island, at on the eastern coast, one will find what is probably the most famous holiday resort on Léros: Alínda with its beautiful beaches. In the recent years, some hotels and other tourist facilities have been established here but Alínda is still unobtrusive and not yet overrun.

The sand and gravel beach, more than one kilometre long, is lined by tamarisks so that there is always sufficient shade.

North of town, one will find several other small bays for swimming, some of which, however, are only accessible over unpaved roads in very poor condition.

North of Parthéni village is the beginning of a large military base. It is here where the island's small airport is situated. The landscape here is rather unfriendly: rocks, dust and barren land. During the time of the military junta the Parthéni camps, which had been constructed by the Italians, gained tragic fame. It was here that numerous political prisoners were held and tortured. However, times have changed and Parthéni is merely a small village today without much significance importance.

Worth visiting nearby is Blefoúti Bay with its gravel beach well suited for children. There is also a tavern serving excellent fish dishes.

The centre of the island's fertile southern regions is Xerókambos. Xerókambos is a sleepy town well suited for quiet holidays even though the gravel beach here is not terribly beautiful. From here, passenger boats depart for Mirtiés on a regular basis (→ *Kálymnos*).

Only a short distance from the docks, one will find the island's only camping area, "Léros Camping" — very green with abundant shade. It is said to be open the entire year.

On the way form Lakkí to Xerókambos, one will pass the large psychiatric asylums of Léros, one of the largest hospitals of this kind in all of Greece. Léros is highly recommended for all those who can do without a lot of activity and who enjoy getting to know the country and its people through small excursions.

Léros / **Practical Information**

Accommodation: The choice of accommodation is abundant with something to suit every taste and budget.

Lakkí: B-category: "Xenon Angelou", doubles priced around £12 ($22), Tel: 02 47/2 25 14.

C-category: "Léros", doubles priced around £10 ($19), Tel: 02 47/2 29 40.

D-category: "Miramare", doubles priced around £8.50 ($15.75), Tel: 02 47/2 20 53, very friendly owner.

In addition, there are several private rooms available.

Agía Marína/Pantéli: "Agía Marína" Guest House, a beautiful house, quietly situated, doubles priced around £8.50 ($15.75).

"Windmill" Guest House, situated directly on the seafront, nice atmosphere, doubles priced around £10 ($19).

E-category: "Rodon", nice house, situated above the bay with very beautiful view, doubles priced around £10 ($19), Tel: 02 47/2 20 75.

"Kavos" Guest House, situated directly along the harbour, a bit noisy but very reasonably priced, doubles around £6,70 ($12.50), Tel: 02 47/2 32 47.

Private rooms are also available in both places.

Alínda: C-category "Irini" Hotel, doubles priced around £15 ($28.50), very clean and well-maintained, Tel: 02 47/2 41 64.

C-category, "Alínda", doubles priced around £13.50 ($25), Tel: 02 47/2 32 66.

C-category, "Maleas Beach", doubles priced around £17 ($31.25), Tel: 02 47/2 33 06 (reservations under 2 28 34).

E-category, "Carina", doubles priced around £8.50 ($15.75), Tel: 02 47/2 27 16.

There are also private rooms available in Alínda and this is also where one will find the only larger hotels on the island.

Xerókambos: There is a camping area near the docks.

Banks: There are banks in Lakkí and in Plátanos. Money can also be exchanged in the travel agencies in Agía Marína.

Beaches: Most beaches on the island are on the eastern coast near Alínda, Agía Marína and Pantéli.

The beaches north of Lakkí Bay on the western coast, those on the northern coast near Parthéni as well as on the southern coast near Xerókambos are also very nice.

Léros (Excursion)

Car and Bicycle Rental: In Lakkí, as well as in Agía Marína and Alínda, bicycles and mopeds can be rented. A car rental agency can be found on the road from Lakkí to Plátanos. Prices for all vehicles are average for Greece. Prices for orientation: cars £23.50 to £34 ($44 to $63) a day, mopeds £6.80 ($12.50) a day, bicycles £2.70 ($5) a day, sometimes negotiating is possible; there are discounts for longer rental periods.

Medical Care: Medical care on Léros is adequate. In Lakkí, as well as in the other larger towns along the east coast, one will find several doctors. The tourist and harbour police in Agía Marína will be able to provide the addresses. There is also a hospital in Lakkí: Tel: 02 47/2 32 51.

Restaurants and Taverns: The choice of restaurants on Léros is abundant and there are some very good taverns. The food is especially good in the following places:

Lakkí: "O Sostos" Tavern next to the post office, very good Greek cuisine, normal prices.

Tavern "Poseidonion", situated on the coastal road, very beautiful terrace and wine is served from the barrel!

Agía Marína: Tavern "Limani", situated directly on the harbour, nice atmosphere, normal prices.

Ouserie "Takamakia", very lively in the evenings, snacks can be ordered together with oúso.

"Esperithes" Restaurant, situated out of town on the road to Alínda. A very special restaurant offering international cuisine in very stylish ambience. Guests are seated in a beautiful garden under age-old orange trees. Very good service, elevated prices.

Pantéli: "Psaropoula" Tavern, situated directly on the seafront; this tavern is said to be the island's best fishing tavern, also serving more unusual fish dishes at fair prices.

"Lotus" Tavern, sometimes even with live music, good Greek cuisine, not the most inexpensive.

Alínda: "O Finkas" Tavern, tables either by the sea or in the garden, good Greek cuisine.

Xerókambos: "Xerókambos" Tavern, directly on the beach, very nice atmosphere, not overcrowded.

Transportation
Air Travel: The island's airport offers the opportunity to fly to Kos or to Rhodes three times a week. The flight to Kos costs around £10 ($19). In addition, there are flights to Athens daily.
Buses on Léros are very scarce, the only bus operating regularly passes all towns on the island about four times a day. There is a relatively elaborate taxi network on the island with pleasantly low prices, Tel: 02 47/2 30 70.
Ferries: Connections by ferry between Léros and Kos are very good; ferries operate on a daily basis. In addition, there are smaller boats departing from Léros to Lípsi, Pátmos, and Kálymnos almost on a daily basis as well.

Important Adresses
Lakkí: The harbour police can be found at the taxi stand, Tel: 02 47/2 22 23.
Post Office: behind the "Leros Palace" Hotel, open 7:30 am to 3 pm, Tel: 02 47/2 25 87.
OTE, directly at the harbour boulevard, Tel: 02 47/2 20 99.
Kastis Travel (ferry tickets), at the taxi stand, Tel: 02 47/2 25 00.
Plátanos/Agía Marína/Pantéli: Tourist and harbour police (simultaneously official tourist information of Léros), at the harbour Agía Marína, Tel: 02 47/2 22 22.
Post Office and OTE: on the road from Plátanos to Agía Marína, Tel: 02 47/2 28 99.
Olympic Airways in Plátanos, Tel: 02 47/2 35 01-4.
Olympic Airways at the airport, Tel: 02 47/2 27 77.
Travel agency Lectec-Travel in Agía Marína, Tel: 02 47/2 34 96 (room reservations for the entire island, excursions etc.).

Linopótis

Linopótis is a small village situated on both sides of the road, halfway between Kos City and → *Andimáchia*. There are no places of interest making a visit to this town a matter of how much time one has to spare.

Maps

The tourist maps of the Greek Toubis Publishing are quite useful and available after arriving on Kos. These will prove quite adequate for orientation and can also be purchased in the form of a "welcome guide" (booklet with map) available at almost all kiosks in Kos City or in the tourist resorts in any shop where souvenirs are sold.

Marmári

Marmári's only real claim to fame is the fact that it is included in the brochures printed by travel organisers. In the winter and off season the town is practically deserted. Near the town, large *salinas* are still in use today and these can be toured.

Accommodation: In Marmári, one will find many of the largest hotels on the island. Most of them are situated on beautiful, long sandy beaches.

Most of these large hotels are regularly booked by package tour organisers, for example, the "Caravia Beach" Hotel, belonging to the A-category, Tel: 02 42/4 12 91 which is one of Kos' best hotels. Here, one can also rent a complete bungalow. The price for a two person bungalow is around £73.50 ($138) per day; the price for a double room in the hotel is around £50 ($94).

Transportation: There is a bus line operating daily to Kos City although not all of the buses go into the village; if Marmári is not the terminal station on the route, the bus will only stop along the main road and the remaining 1½ kilometres (about 1 mile) to the village must be covered on foot.

Mastichári

Mastichári is a small town situated on the northern coast of the island, about 30 kilometres (19 miles) from Kos City.

The village has approximately 100 residents who have adapted themselves well to tourists. This can be seen by the number of new buildings in town. However, Mastichári is still recommended as a destination on Kos' northern coast because one will still find only small hotels, guest houses, and private rooms here and the beaches are not yet overrun. The view of the neighbouring island of → *Kálymnos* is also very nice. An excursion to the ruis of the early Christian basilica Ag. Joánnis near the village can also be recommended.

The taverns of Mastichári are said to serve the best fish dishes on the island. The "Kalí Kardía" Tavern can be recommended for good fish dishes at reasonable prices.

The beach of Mastichári runs for several kilometres on both sides of town and even has sections with sand dunes.

Because the north wind always makes for strong waves, the beach is not well suited for children but is a virtual paradise for windsurfers. Surfboards can be rented at the beach.

Accommodation: B-category "Mastichári Beach", Tel: 02 42/5 13 71, doubles priced around £13.50 ($25).

E-category: "Andreas", Tel: 02 42/5 15 56-7, doubles priced around £9 ($16).

E-category: "Zevgas", Tel: 02 42/2 25 77, doubles priced around £9 ($16). There are also private rooms to rent.

Transportation: There is a bus line operating regularly from Mastichári to Kos City. In addition, it takes only 50 minutes by ferry to reach Kálymnos from here.

Medication → *Pharmacies*

Medical Care

Due to the high number of tourists, medical care on Kos is excellent both in terms of the facilities available and the quality of treatment. After all, the island does have a long and prestigious medical tradition to maintain: in ancient times, Kos was world-famous through the Asclepius Sanctuary and its founder → *Hippocrates,* who brought the most significant medical school of antiquity into existence.

There are an ample number of well-equipped medical practices in Kos City, Kardámaena, and in Kéfalos, with western European standards, although first impressions might sometimes be misguiding. Most doctors have studied in Athens or even abroad and therefore speak at least one foreign language, usually English.

In Greece, it is normal to pay directly for medical treatment and any medication. Invoices can then be submitted later to the health insurance company which will reimburse the expenses. If unsure whether insurance includes protection abroad, it is recommended to take out supplementary health insurance for the duration of one's stay on Kos.

The address of the hospital is: General Hippocratic Hospital, Odos Ippokrates 32, Kos City.

Monasteries

There are no monasteries worth mentioning on Kos; however, on the neighboring islands, one will find monasteries very much worth seeing

Numerous details that catch the eye — a monastery on the neighbouring island of Kálymnos

(→ *individual entries*). Since many of the monasteries are no longer inhabited, farmers' families are often responsible for their care and maintenance. In return, they are allowed to use the buildings. The Greek Orthodox Church does not have enough money ensure the preservation of such monasteries. Before visiting a monastery, it is always a good idea to ask in nearest village whether it is open and, in case it is closed, who is in charge of the keys and who responsible for the monastery might have to be present during the visit.

There are usually charming stories in connection with the establishment of these monasteries which the keepers enjoy telling visitors on such occasions. One should never fortet to make a small voluntary contribution after such a visit since the money is desperately needed for the preservation and maintenance of the monastery. Generally, the most important sight in the monasteries is the church containing numerous smaller and large treasures (→ *Icons*).

Even most of the smaller churches are locked and will only be opened upon request. Here too, the visitor should at least donate some money for candles.

Money

Bringing Greek drachmas into the country is limited to 100,000 drachmas per person; the export is limited to 20,000 per person. However, it is a much better idea to change only a small amount of money before the trip because exchange rates in Greece are much more favourable. Bank notes of 5,000 drachmas are not allowed to be brought into or out of the country at all. There are no restrictions whatsoever with regard to the import or export of foreign currencies. However, amounts exceeding £535 ($1,000) should be declared when coming to the country because otherwise these currencies may not be officially taken out of the country upon departure.

The Greek inflation rate is rapidly on the increase — so much so, that the drachma lost about 50% of its value between 1988 and 1993. For the tourist, the inflation rates compensates for some of the drastic price increases but the local residents suffer a great deal under these circumstances. The inflation also explains why the normal Greek citizen is so interest in "hard" currencies such as the US dollar or the German mark. It possible to change money everywhere privately — and this at the official exchange rate which one should definitely investigate beforehand. There are practically no black market rates.

Although these private exchange opportunities are much more convenient, especially when considering that the business hours of banks are rather short, the official exchange receipts are demanded on occasion when leaving the country. For this reason, one should be sure to keep these receipts.

The general business hours for banks are from Monday to Thursday from 8 am to 1:30 pm, Friday 7:45 am to 1:30 pm. Some banks are also open in the afternoon, but only for currency exchange. These business hours may vary slightly. Traveller's cheques which usually have a slightly more favourable exchange rate can only be exchanged in banks or certain travel agencies.

Credit cards are accepted in most shops in tourist areas. The most widely accepted cards are American Express and Eurocard but Diner's Club and Visa are also accepted. It also possible to have money transferred to every Greek post office (the maximum amount per transfer is about £2.400/$4,500). Smaller towns and remote islands very often do not have a bank. Here, one will be able to exchange money or cheques at the post office.

Mythology

There is hardly an island or a city in Greece whose early history or development is not inseparably interconnected with Greek mythology. Here legends, rumours, reality, and the past mesh into a colourful conglomeration.

Many of these legends are still kept alive today and commemorated on every possible occasion.

The origin of each and every ancient site, small temple, monastery and chapel contains components from mythology and legends. And it is precisely this that makes not only Kos but almost any other place and any other island in Greece so enthralling.

Kos is linked to the mythological King Meropos who is said to have had a daughter named Koos after whom the island was named. What is certain is that the name is in fact derived from the linguistic tradition of Asia Minor.

Nísyros *(Excursion)*

The volcanic island of Nísyros is located only few nautical miles (travel time: 2½ hours) south of Kos and is easily accessible *(→ Nísyros / Transportation)*. The landscape on Nísyros is certainly one of the most surprising in all of the Aegean.

The entire island actually consists of an extinct volcanic crater, 700 metres (2,290 feet) above sea level. Thanks to the absorbant lava and pumice which stores water like a sponge, Nísyros is a relatively fertile island; its profile is green with marvellous white, sandy beaches and some truly beautiful villages.

The *volcanic crater* (caldéra) is used agriculturally in part and also offers vistas reminiscent of lunar landscapes. Even today, toxic sulphur vapours even today escape from the earth in some places; these can cause headaches and nausea if inhaled too deeply. The air smells of rotten eggs and the landscape unfolds in all shades of yellow and red.

One should not miss seeing Nísyros and definitely try to fit in more time than just one day. It is well worth it.

Nísyros / **Mandráki**

Mandráki, the main town on the island is a bizarre place. At first, it seems rather hostile because the houses have no windows facing the sea, giving a closed impression and there is no typically Greek Paralía (harbour boulevard). It is very unusual for a Greek harbour town to "turn its back" on the sea.

Nísyros (Excursion)

Similarly unusual is the fact that Mandráki has no protected harbour so that if the sea is not perfectly calm, ships have difficulties landing here. Entering the village when coming from the mole, one will immediately be enchanted by the charms and atmosphere of this place. Whitewashed houses with colourful flowers, small alleyways, and beautifully ornamented balconies convey a warm and friendly impression.

Women sit in front of their houses enjoying a chat, small shops in the narrow alleyways draw shoppers, taverns offer truly excellent cuisine — all in all, a comfortable place one can really feel good. In addition to the abundance of beautiful houses, the *Folklore Museum* near the town hall at the central Platía is worth visiting. It is within a private building and displays traditional costumes and objects of daily use from Nísyros. Unfortunately, the times it is open are very irregular.

The entire village is dominated by the remnants of the *Knights of St. John*'s *Fortress* built in 1315; which should not be missed. At the beginning of the Kastro (fortress) rock which is not very high but rather steep, one will find the *Church of St. Mary Panagías tis Spilianís* from around 1600. It is linked to numerous stories regarding the island. The view of the vast blue sea from here and the intricate pattern of Mandráki's snow-white houses is truly unique. Farther above the village, one will find the ruins of the *Acropolis* formerly a part of the ancient upper city. The way up there is, however, rather tiring because it leads through some rather rugged sections.

Even today one can admire some of the most impressive walls in all of Greece, the so-called *Cyclopean Walls* from the Dorian Age (→ *History*). They consist of giant stone blocks stacked upon each other, evoking the question in every visitor how the people of those times managed to tap the energy necessary to accomplish this.

From here, one may also enjoy the beautiful view of Mandráki.

Nísyros / **Excursions on the Island**

The most interesting excursion on the island is most defiitely a trip to the *volcanic crater* (Caldéra). On the way to it, one will pass some beautiful villages and beaches.

Only a few kilometres east of Mandráki is **Loutrá**, the island's former *thermal baths* from 1872. Today, hot springs still bubble up from the ground. After this facility had completely fallen into decay, it is now being restored with rather modest means. It is here, where one can find a very beautiful beach with almost white pumice sand.

The next place one will reach is **Páli**, a small fishing village with a cozy atmosphere very suitable for a holiday in the country. In Páli, fishermen still live from the sea and, with some luck, it could be possible to go along with one of them on his daily fishing trip. There are some good taverns in the village, serving excellent fish dishes. To the east of the village one can find small and rather secluded beaches along with a second *thermal bath complex* built in 1895. It is presently being reconstructed as well.

Emborió and **Nikiá** are two beautiful small villages situated in the island's centre, high up on the side of the crater. Unfortunately, they are almost empty, populated only by very few older people these days. Life does pick up a little during the summer months.

Near **Emborió**, one can find two beautiful old monasteries, the *Taxiarchis Monastery* and the *Kirás Monastery*. Both are located within good walking distance. The *Kirás Monastery* has an especially beautiful inner courtyard with numerous plants. Neither of the monasteries are inhabited any longer.

Owing to its geographic location at 430 metres (1,406 feet) above sea level, the small village of **Nikiá** is certainly one of the most beautiful villages in all of the Dodecanese. The view of the blue Aegean waters on the one hand and the Caldéra on the other hand is truly breathtaking. On clear days, the sweeping panorama extends all the way to the island of Tílos and the mountains of Rhodes. From Nikiá, an good trail leads into the volcanic crater (Caldéra).

Nikiá is a pretty village with whitewashed houses and a small, cozy central Platía. Unfortunately, there are no beaches at Nikiá. If one is lucky, and manages to rent one of the few private rooms here, it is very easy to be quickly integrated into the village community.

The *Caldéra* comprises a landscape which one would not be expect of a Greek island. The ground was in part transformed into fertile agricultural land; the remainder is still a barren lunar landscape. One almost feels

Nísyros (Excursion)

as if in Iceland: mudpots boil and bubble and foul-smelling sulphur vapours waft over the landscape.

Although the volcano has not been active for more than hundred years, minor tremors shake the area regularly. The last earthquake in 1933 also greatly affected Kos, causing heavy damage. The crater's diameter is around 260 metres (850 feet) with a depth of around 30 metres (100 feet).

Nísyros / **Practical Information**

Accommodation: Changes in recent years have improved the situation considerably. There are very beautiful private rooms available in Mandráki — the tourist police will be of assitance in locating them.

Accommodation is also offered in hotels:

B-category: "Charitos", doubles priced around £12 ($22), Tel: 02 42/3 13 22, situated along the road to Páli.

C-category: "Porfyris", doubles priced around £13.50 ($25), Tel: 02 42/3 13 76, a rather modern hotel with an own small swimming pool.

D-category: "Three Brothers", doubles priced around £8.50 ($15.75), Tel: 02 42/3 13 44, situated directly at the docks; recommended.

C-category: "White Beach", doubles priced around £17 ($31.50), the only larger hotel on the island, situated directly at the beach.

E-category: "Drossia", doubles priced around £6.70 ($12.50), Tel: 02 42/3 13 28, a small guest house in the middle of the town.

E-category: "Paraskevi Mammi", doubles priced around £8.50 ($15.75), Tel: 02 42/3 14 35, situated in Páli; highly recommended.

Banks: Money can be exchanged in a shop at the central Platía, the small travel agency, at the post office and at the landing point for the ferries. Up to present, there is no bank on Nísyros.

Beaches: Despite its volcanic origin, the island does not have typical black volcanic beaches, but instead, very beautiful white beaches of pumice sand. Mandráki itself has no beaches. The best beaches are located on the road to Páli and farther to the east.

Car Rental: There is no car rental agency on Nísyros but an agency at Mandráki rents out mopeds priced around £6.70 ($12.50) per day.

Medical Care
There is a doctor in Mandráki (Tel: 02 42/3 12 17). In difficult cases, a helicopter is ordered from Kos City.

Restaurants
All of the island's taverns make a good impression, the quality of the food is excellent, and the prices are reasonable. Here are a few of them:

Right at the beginning of the village: "Tsardaki" Tavern, a rather simple tavern with average prices.

"Franzis" Tavern in the upper part of the town, rather crowded during the day rather by day tourists but still recommended: good food and not to mention very nice seats.

There are several more taverns which one should not hesitate to try.

Shopping
Except for a piece of pumice stone, there is not much which would count as a typical souvenir from Nísyros. Thus, there are no typical tourist shops in Mandráki or on the rest of the island. All articles for daily use can be obtained, however, without any problems.

Transportation
There is *bus service* to all areas on the island from Mandráki twice daily. Furthermore, there is a bus for excursions to the volcanic crater. Departure times depend on the arrival of the excursion boats.

There are also a number of *taxis* on the island, although this is by no means an inexpensive option.

The *ferries* between Kos and Nísyros are very good. There are daily excursion boats from Kos City / Kardámaena to Nísyros and during the summer ferries operating at least four times a week. The duration of the trip is about $2\frac{1}{2}$ hours.

Important Adresses
Tourist Police: directly at the harbour of Mandráki; also tourist information.

Harbour Police: at the harbour office, Tel: 02 42/3 12 22.

Post Office: at the harbour office.

OTE: on the road from the harbour into town, follow the signs.

Travel Agency: at the town hall; airline reservations can be made here as well.

Nudism

Officially speaking, nudism is forbidden on Kos as in the rest of Greece. However, on most of the island's larger beaches, topless bathing is the rule although it should be limited to the beach sections belonging to hotels.

There are family beaches on Kos, visited predominantly by Greek families. Here consideration for the customs of the host country is appropriate; women should refraim from bathing topless.

Particularly in the western portions of the island, one will find sufficient secluded beach sections, making it possible to bathe with a much less restrictive "dress code".

Olympic Airways

Domestic flights in Greece are only offered by the partially state-run airline Olympic Airways.

Although it is possible to book domestic flights in Greece from abroad but it is safer and much less expensive to do so in Greece.

Either way, reservations are highly recommended because, due to the low prices, the flights are usually completely booked.

Olympic Airways Offices
Athens: Syngrou Avenue 96, Tel: 01/9 29 21 11; at Sintagma square, Tel: 01/9 29 22 47; and at the Olympic Airways terminals at the Athens airport.

Kos: Od. Vasílios Konstantinou 22, Tel: 02 42/2 83 31 and at the airport terminal on Kos, Tel: 02 42/5 12 29.

Flights
The following are domestic flights from Kos to other Greek destinations: 2-3 times daily to Athens, 3-4 times weekly to Léros, 5 times weekly to Rhodes, once a week to Thessaloníki, once a week to Sámos.

OTE → *Telephones*

Palaiópyli (Old Pylí)

Palaiópyli is located only a few kilometres from the town of → *Pylí*. Palaiópyli is deserted and mostly in ruins but its location does make a trip worthwhile.
Old Pylí is dominated by the ruins of a *fortress* and the town is home to three old *Byzantine churches* with in part well-preserved frescoes. The churches are said to originate from the 11th century.

Pátmos *(Excursion)*

Actually, Pátmos is situated too far away for a day-trip from Kos; since the island is absolutely worth seeing, several days should be set aside for a visit. No luxury ship exists which does not drop anchor at Pátmos and in summer, thousands of visitors arrive here every day. The *St. John's Monastery (→ Pátmos/Monastery Agios Ioánnis Theologos)* and the *Grotto of the Secret Revelation* attract crowds of visitors. This is probably the most famous monastery in Greece and definitely worth seeing.
Apart from this, the island also offers unusually beautiful sights: Chóra counts among the most beautiful towns in the Dodecanese, although the entire island sooner makes a cycladic impression with its numerous bays, beautiful beaches and lively harbour towns.
Those who come to visit Pátmos should take some time to discover the beauties of the island despite the masses of tourists. Moreover, the size of the island makes it possible to explore even the most remote areas on foot.

Pátmos / **Skála and Chóra**

Both towns Skála and Chóra have almost grown together and give an unforgettable impression to travellers arriving by ship.
The white houses of the harbour town are situated at the end of a deep bay. Life pulsates here on top of the mountain; on the left, the mighty *Agios Ioánnis Monestary* is perched above the snow-white houses of Chóra nestled on the mountain slope as if searching for protection.

Arriving at the harbour is an unforgettable event, especially at night when the monastery is illuminated.

There are numerous taverns and bars in Skála as well as a broad selection of accommodation. One must go to the north or the south of town to find the beaches since there are no beaches in Skála itself.

Despite the vast number of visitors, the town still possesses an inviting atmosphere. The style of the houses, even the newer buildings, seems very natural and no skyscrapers or strangely shaped new buildings disturbs the overall impression.

The town is ideal for a longer stay — from here, one can visit a different bay every day.

A serpentine road or the old stairway leads to Chóra; visitors will find themselves in a completely different world. It seems that the immense monastery in the immediate vicinity has such a strong effect that life does not take place in the alleyways but in the small inner courtyards, rather atypical for Greece.

The entire town is beautiful with all the houses in excellent condition. Small, and narrow alleyways run through the town, punctuated with small Platías (squares). Chóra is probably one of the most beautiful island villages in the entire Aegean.

Many manor houses testify to the island's former affluence. One of them, the *Simandiri House* can be toured.

The town's main attraction and the island's most important sight is of course the *Agíos Ioánnis Theológos Monestary* which seems like a knight's castle with its strong, fortified walls.

Pátmos / **The Agíos Ioánnis Theológos Monastery**

The monastery was founded in 1088 by the abbot Christódoulos on the same sit where the Temple of Artemis stood in ancient times. In the course of the centuries, the monastery was to undergo many power struggles in the eastern Mediterranean, but always managed to safeguard its independence and with this, a certain privileged status for the entire island of Pátmos.

Although the monastery ranks among the richest of all monasteries in Greece even today, it is dependent on tourism for its income.

The valuable *library* with countless very old manuscripts (among others, copies of St. Mark's Gospel from the 6th century) is worthwhile seeing. By current evaluation, these manuscripts are inconceivably valuable. Of course, one should not miss a visit to the *treasure chamber* where one can admire more than 200 icons and 600 chasubles embroidered with gold and silver.

On the rooftop terrace of the monastery, one can enjoy a unique panorama of the entire island extencint all the way to Léros, Kálymnos and, on clear days, even Kos; one of the most beautiful views in the entire Mediterranean.

The hours that the monasteryis open vary. Generally, the monastery is open in the morning from 8 to noon and again in the afternoon after lunch. The admission fee to the treasure chamber is around 85p ($1.60). Those interested in art and history will be able to buy interesting pamphlets on Pátmos.

Pátmos / **Excursions on the Island**

There are some very beautiful beaches in the southeast of the island. Here, the village of **Gríko** is gradually developing into an important holiday resort.

The Gríko's beach is lined by tamarisks and a small island off the coast gives the bay the appearance of a lake. The surf is very calm, making this beach especially well-suited for children.

Farther south, individual secluded bays are accessible over roadways in very poor condition.

The island's most beautiful beach, the **Psilí Amos** (fine sand) is also situated here, but is not that easy to reach. In summer, there is a ferry connection from Skála and the tavern there is also open.

The bay of Melói is an attractive destination the island's north and is within good walking distance from Skála. The gravel and sand beach is pleasantly shady and it is here where Pátmos' camping area is located.

Farther to the north, it becomes quieter again, and here, one will find the only settlement in the island's northern regions: **Kámpos**. Probably owing to its remote location on the island, it has preserved very much of its original character. There are only very few tourists here and private rooms are available. A very interesting beach can be found on the northern tip of the island: Lámbi Bay.

Exposed to northern winds in summer, Lámbi Bay is actually not very appropriate swimming but it is an Eldorado for those interested in minerals. Colourful stones of all hues can be found here. Moreover, one can enjoy an almost deserted landscape and unlimited tranquillity.

Pátmos / **Practical Information**

Accommodation

A very wide selection of accommodation is available, supplemented by private rooms in Skála, Chóra, and Kámpos.

Skála/Chóra

B-category: "Skala", doubles priced around £18.50 ($35), a very comfortable hotel directly at the harbour, Tel: 02 47/3 13 43.

B-category: "Patmion", Emm. Xenou 34, doubles priced between £8.50 ($15.75) and £10 ($19), reasonably priced, Tel: 02 47/3 13 13.

C-category: "Galini", doubles priced around £12 ($22), Tel: 02 47/3 12 40.

C-category: "Hellinis", pleasant house, doubles priced around £10 ($19), Tel: 02 47/3 12 75.

D-category: "Rodon", doubles priced around £8.50 ($15.75), Tel: 02 47/3 13 71.

D-category: "Diethnes", doubles priced around £6.70 ($12.50), Tel: 02 47/3 13 57.

The *camping area* is situated on Melói Bay; very clean and shady, highly recommended. Even for travellers without tent who are also welcome here although the camping area is completely overrun in summer. Open from April to October, Tel: 02 47/3 18 21 or 3 17 54. Price per person and tent: around £2.20 ($4).

In *Chóra* there are no hotels. However, private rooms are available *(→ Tourist Information)*.

Gríko

B-category: "Artemis", doubles priced around £12 ($22), Tel: 02 47/3 15 55.

B-category: "Grikos", doubles priced around £12 ($22), Tel: 02 47/3 15 55.

D-category: "Fliesvos", pleasant atmosphere, doubles priced around £10 ($19), Tel: 3 13 80.

The "Dolphin" Hotel in the very north of the island on Lámbi Bay is very beautiful. It is nestled in vineyards and very quiet; doubles priced around £10 ($19), Tel: 02 47/3 10 72.

Banks: There is a branch office of the National Bank of Greece directly on the harbour square in Skála (open 8 am to 2 pm). Travel agencies will also exchange money at the official exchange rate.

Beaches: There are several bays with beaches on Pátmos, although most of them are gravel. The most important ones are along the northern coastline, on Melói Bay and in the south at Gríko Bay. All others bays are

In addition to the world famous Asclepius Sanctuary, there are numerous other archaeological excavations on Kos

easily accessible from Skála on foot; walking there will take one to two hours.

Car and Motorcycle Rental: At present, only mopeds and motorbikes are available on Pátmos. Prices per day range from around £5 ($9.50) to £6.80 ($12.50) at Makis-Tours in Skála, located north of the harbour, Tel: 02 47/3 15 08.

Medical Care: Medical care on Pátmos is good. There are several doctors in Skála (Tel: 02 47/3 15 77) well prepared for the vast number of visitors.

Restaurants

The selection is very diverse; some tips:

"Pirofáni" Tavern in Skála offers fish specialities at reasonable prices.

"O Grigóris" Tavern in Skála, at the mole, always quite crowded, the food is excellent with a wide selection.

"Pandélis" Tavern in Skála, on the parallel street to the harbour boulevard. Good Greek cuisine at very reasonable prices.

"Olimbia" Tavern in Chóra at Platía Agía Levia — should not be visited during the day because of the masses of patrons; highly recommended for an evening meal.

"Vangelis" Tavern in Chóra at Platía Agía Levia. A favourite meeting point, also highly recommended, although not exactly cheap.

"Pirgos" Tavern at the entrance to Chóra, very stylish, beautiful view from the terrace. Medium price range.

"Giórgos" Tavern in Chóra, average prices, good food and very friendly service.

Transportation

Buses: All important points on Pátmos are served regularly by the bus system. The bus stop in Skála is in front of the harbour office.

Ferries: Pátmos is very well integrated into the ferry network. There are ferries departing daily to Kos/Rhodes/Piraeus. To Kos/Rhodes there are also the fast hydrofoils called "Flying Dolphins". In addition, ferry service is also offered to Sámos and the Northern Aegean Islands three times a week. There is even a direct ferry to Venice once a week, although this is not the least expensive travel option. Daily excursions to the neighboring islands are also offered.

Taxis: There are some rather inexpensive taxis on the island.
Important Adresses: EOT tourist information, directly at the harbour, Tel: 02 47/3 11 58 or 3 16 66.
Tourist police: like EOT, Tel: 02 47/3 10 00.
Post office: directly beside the tourist information, Tel: 02 47/3 13 16.
OTE: in the town's centre, the way to the main square is guided by signs, Tel: 02 47/3 13 99.

The People of Kos

Alhough Kos ranks third in size in the Dodecanese after Rhodes and Kárpathos, it only has a population of around 17,000, 8,000 of which live in the capital Kos City. The rest is scattered mainly among ten other towns. Apart from the tourist industry large proportions of the population work in agriculture, farming olives, grapes and citrus fruits.

The residents of Kos have never been great seafarers, they have close ties to their island and try to make their living from agriculture and commerce.

Despite the high level of tourism, the people, particularly in the small mountain villages in the → *Díkeos* are very close to their island and cultivate many old traditions. Unfortunately however, more and more concessions are made for tourism as can be clearly seen in Kos City and the typical tourist resorts on the northern and southern coasts.

The island Kos does not suffer from a diminishing population as do many other Greek islands. However, particularly the young people turn their backs on the island during the winter months. In summer, they try to make a living from the island's tourism but in winter, they take refuge in the big cities on the mainland. Thus, a new generation of farmers is lacking on the island. More and more, fields remain untended, orchards are not harvested and in the end, the farms must be given up completely. Up to present, the social structure in most of the villages is still intact but whoever passes through the island's interior with an observant eye will see mostly older people passing the time in the Kafenío. Tradition and progress collide here head-on; progress that was simply to quick and seems to have taken Kos by surprise.

The people of Kos are quite friendly and open-minded towards strangers but this natural friendliness is increasingly motivated by a healthy business sense.

Still it will happen over and over again that one is awarded with friendly smiles when merely trying to speak a few words of Greek. This especially makes the older village residents happy.

The question remains where Kos' development will lead, even though most of these changes can be observed virtually everywhere. Up to now, the residents are still not financially dependent and the island's economy is self-sufficient. However, if the developments continue on their present course, then international investors in the tourism sector could take over the island and its residents, degrading them to servants on their own island.

During the warm nights, one can sit outside for hours listening to music and chatting with the locals

Períptero

Like the Kafenío it is impossible to image Greek streets without a kiosk, the *Períptero*. These are like small supermarkets, offering just about everything one might need in addition to cigarettes and newspapers. Often, they are open until very late at night and are the place one can buy anything at this time. It is also possible to use the telephone at almost every kiosk. This is only slightly more expensive than at the OTE. The red telephones are for regional calls, whereas the grey telephones are for internationals calls (strangely enough, the lines here are often better than at the telephone office.)

Those who enjoy photography will not have any difficulties finding plenty of photographic motifs in Greece

Pharmacies

Greek pharmacies usually offer a wide selection of products including most of the well-known international brands. This is also true for pharmacies on Kos. Generally, medications, even prescription medication must be paid for in cash. It is a good idea to ask for a receipt which should be kept for reimbursement from the health insurance company. All medication can be purchased without a prescription usually at a lower price than in central Europe. The addresses of pharmacies are mentioned in the descriptions of the towns. An adequate number of pharmacies can be found in Kos City as well as in most larger towns on the island. In Kos City, there is even a pharmacy with 24-hour service.

Photography / Video

Film and other photographic materials be found in almost any town on Kos, although prices are rather high. For this reason, it is a good idea to bring along sufficient material for the trip; another reason is that some of the film sold on the island is old — be sure to check the expiration date. The best time for taking pictures is the morning and late afternoon. Around midday, it is a good idea to use a UV-filter because of the strong rays of the sun.

As a rule, local residents do not mind having their picture taken but one should still be tactful and not start a shooting session without warning. A gracious smile or a questioning expression can sometimes help work small miracles. It is prohibited to take pictures of military facilities and bases which are marked with signs with a red margin and a slash through a camera.

Particularly on the Dodecanese islands, there is a lot of military presence that strictly guards the observance of these regulations.

Videotapes for a camcorder (mostly VHS-C and video 8) should be brought along from home. They are meanwhile available on Kos but only at very high prices.

Postal System

A post office can be found in almost every village on Kos. They are responsible for all postal matters from letters to parcels. Mail can be received at post offices by general delivery and it is also possible to wire money (maximum amount £2,400/$4,400).

Business hours for post offices vary considerably (→ *individual entries*). It is not possible to place phonecalls at Greek post offices. This is the domain of another organisation, the OTE (→ *Telephones*). It is also possible to place phonecalls at most of the kiosks (→ *Períptero*).

Psérimos *(Excursion)*

Psérimos is a tiny island exactly halfway between Kos and Kálymnos. Excursion to Psérimos are offered from Kos City (more details in the travel agencies at Kos City). Psérimos is still a very quiet island with roughly 100 residents, a very small village and no cars. The only beach on the island is located right near the village and some accommodation can be found here as well.

Psérimos almost conveys the feeling that progress have completely passed by without a trace, if disregarding the military base in the eastern portions of the island.

One can take walks on the island that will lead to a natural spring or to a village which was already abandoned 150 years ago. Apart from that, one can also merely enjoy uncomplicated life in the small village. It is quite astonishing to see the different worlds separated only by a straight 5 kilometres (about 3 miles) in width. On the one side, cosmopolitan Kos and the other side, the almost forgotten Psérimos.

Accommodation: There is an astonishing number of private rooms available on Psérimos. Reservations can be made at the central room service under the telephone number 02 43/2 31 95. Also recommedned: "Tripolitis" Hotel Tel: 02 43/2 31 96, situated directly on the small beach.

Transportation: Excursions are offered from Kos City (for details contact the travel agencies in Kos City). There is a ferry to the island once a week. There are also daily connections by boat so that one can also island hop.

Pylí

Pylí is a small village in the fertile plain on the northern slope of the → *Dikeos*. It is one of the most authentic villages on Kos and has almost 1,500 inhabitants.

The regions surrounding the village are very fertile, fresh water from a spring provides the village with water throughout the year. The *well house* originates from the year 1592. The Kafeníon next to the spring is beautiful.

From Pylí, one has the opportunity to visit the abandoned village → *Plaiópyli* or Old Pylí. There are small taverns to provide for the physical well-being of the visitors.

Accommodation: Private rooms are available in a modest number. It is best to ask in one of the taverns.

The arrival of Asclepius on the island — this beautiful mosaic can be seen in the museum of Kos

Transportation: The town can be reached by a bus operating daily from Kos City.

Public Transport → *Travel on Kos*

Religion

Almost 97% of the population are members of the Greek Orthodox Church, the rest are Jewish, Moslem, Roman Catholic and of other faiths. The Greek Orthodox Church — an independent church from the orthodox community — still plays a very important role in the life of the individual as well as society. The Papás is omnipresent. At least in rural regions and on most of the islands, one will hardly find anybody who did

Where tourists now dominate the picture was once the workplace of the famous physician Hippocrates

not marry in the Church and does not attend mass on at least important holidays.

Even on secular holidays, the Papás will often be found in the first row when a wreath is laid or the dead are honoured.

Church and religion still characterise the image of Greece for travellers; be it the priests with their long hair and beards, or the old people in the bus, crossing themselves when passing by a church. And, of course, church interiors also contribute to this. It is here where the tourist becomes completely aware that he or she is in a country with a different dominant Christian church, the Orthodox Catholic and Apostolic Church of the East.

Masses, where tourists can take part without any problems, differ very much from other churches. The rites are very old and antiphonal singing determines the overall acoustic impression.

The sermon plays only a minor role in the Orthodox Church. The whole service is less dedicated to the believers than to praising the heavenly forces.

Somebody once wrote the words "Those who takes part in the liturgy is drawn and integrated into this reality and can leave the world behind... The more mysterious the liturgy, the more certain it is not of this world. Visitors who find masses in Greece old-fashioned and very strange will have to understand that mystery is the vital element of this religion."

Other differences are that the confession has almost no significance and that the Julian calender instead of the Gregorian is still used. Therefore, most moving holidays like Easter and Pentecost are usually on different dates from when other Christian churches celebrate them.

And there are some differences with regard to what is believed:

For the Orthodox Christian, purgatory does not exist and the Holy Spirit only comes from God the Father and not the Son. The sovereignty of the Pope is not accepted and, of course, he is not considered infallible with regard to doctrines.

Restaurants → *Cuisine, individual entries*

Shopping

Because of the fact that Kos, like some other Dodecanese islands, is subject to special customs regulations, alcohol and tobacco are very inexpensive here.

Of course, shops in Kos City and in many other places on the island will offer articles for daily use, but here and there one will still find shops that stand out (→ *Kos City*).

Souvenirs worthwhile mentioning and, of course, buying are:
— leather goods, some of which are nicely hand worked;
— ceramics, some of which are very fine reconstructions of their antique prototypes; and
— icons, in part very tasteful imitations of antique or well-known icons.

The possibilities for cooking on one's own are very good. Markets always offer fresh fruits and vegetables and some of the products even originate from Kos. Grocers and supermarkets can be found in every town. In the mountain villages of Kos, visitors can often find fresh herbs and teas which are highly recommended. A cup of sage tea brewed from freshly picked leaves can sometimes perform miracles.

Sights

It is impossible to mention all sights of Kos and its neighbouring islands; there are simply too many. References to specific sights are consistently given under the appropriate entries in this guide.

The most important and most famous sight on Kos is the → *Asclepius Sanctuary* which can be counted to the most beautiful sights of the Dodecanese. Furthermore, the *St. John's Monastery* on the island of → *Pátmos* enjoys international fame so that a visit there is highly recommended.

A magnificent landscape is unique throughout the Greek islands is the volcanic island of → *Nísyros* with its *Caldéra* (volcanic crater) and villages which almost hang on the mountain slopes.

Speed Limits

The same speed limits as on the Greek mainland apply for Kos: 100 km/h (63 mph) are permitted for cars on expressways (irrelevant because there aren't any on Kos), 80 km/h (50 mph) on normal roads, and 70 km/h (44mph) for motorcycles. Within villages or towns, its is 50 km/h (32 mph) for cars and 40 km/h (25 mph) for motorcycles. However, it is recommended to drive rather slowly and carefully on Kos because a road in relatively good condition may suddenly turn into a gravel road or be strewn with potholes, or the road may be blocked by fallen rocks.

Sponges

Only 100 years ago, there were numerous sponge divers in the southern Dodecanese and entire islands made a living from this branch of economy. However, it was a very dangerous field of work since the men dove more than 30 metres deep holding their breath. There were many accidents and the extreme water pressure at these depths caused severe health problems. With technical progress, the diving depths became increasingly deeper and the Aegean Sea was virtually plundered. Since not only the supply of natural sponges declined, but the demand for natural sponges as well, this meant the economic decay for the islands. Some of the island have only recovered from this blow with the money earned through tourism.

→ *Kálymnos* is the only remaining Greek island that still has a sponge fleet. Every year in April, the ships leave the harbour and this event is celebrated with a large public festival. But even today the relatives have to fear that not all men will return safe and sound. The ships remain at sea for almost half a year because they must meanwhile go to different regions all over the world.

When the sponge divers return with their ships in October to the harbour of Póthia, this event is also celebrated. The sponge divers and their families have to live from the earnings from the sponges until the next spring.

If keeping this background in mind when buying a sponge, one will see theat the prices for the sponges are quite justified. Some of the shops not only sell the sponges but also deomonstrate how a rather ugly brown lump is turned into a valuable bathing sponge.

Sports and Recreation

The only organised types of sport on Kos are aquaticwater sports.
Windsurfing: The conditions for windsurfing are especially good on the northern coast. Here, the large hotels offer numerous options for renting equipment. Since the sea is rather rough at times, a certain level of competence in this sport is required. Overschmid International's surfing station at Marmári Beach is highly recommended, also offering lessons for beginners. Prices are around £6.70 ($12.50) an hour. Otherwise, the southern coast is better suited to beginners.

The sponge divers return in October with their catch — a scene from the harbour of Póthia on the island of Kálymnos

Waterskiing: Those who like waterskiing should definitely visit the southern coast near Kardámaena and Kéfalos. Larger hotels will be able to provide the necessary equipment.

Tennis: All larger international hotels have their own tennis courts.

Cycling: Being a rather flat island, Kos is quite suitable for bicycle trips. Owing to this, the selection bicycle rental agencies is enormous → *Kos City / Practical Information*.

Symi *(Excursion)*

Symi is one of the most beautiful islands of the Dodecanese. The arrival at the harbour of Symi resembles an Aegean dream, and without any exaggeration, Symi's harbour and capital city can be regarded as one of the most beautiful places in all of Greece.

At the end of the deep and narrow bay, colourful houses with red tile roofs scale the slope — a unique symphony of colours.

One will also discover numerous *manor houses,* dating back to the golden age of sponge diving. In those times, Symi was one of the main centres for Greek sponge fishing.

However, like on many other islands, numerous people migrated from Symi so that the town which had a population of more than 20,000 about 100 years ago, is home to only around 3,000 residents today. In those days, many ships from Symi travelled as far as north Africa.

Simultaneous with the decline of the island, many of the magnificent houses fell into decayed until the island was rediscovered by tourism in the late 70s. Meanwhile, tourism has become the most important economic factor and restoration of many of these manor houses (Archontiká = distinguished houses) has begun. Some are being converted into spacious holiday apartments.

Entering the harbour, one already can see the town's landmark from quite a distance: the *clock tower* from 1881.

This marks the beginning of the busy *Paralía* which surrounds almost the entire harbour. Shops, taverns, and restaurants are concentrated in this area. The town's strong orientation towards tourism is very apparent here, but a very particular charm and atmosphere still remain. Forming a backdrop for the harbour is the city hall an the Platía (square) — the actual centre of the lower city which has grown together with the upper city. Both parts of the city are connected by a seemingly endless stairway, the Kali Stráta (= good street). All told, there are more than 300 steps. Whereas tourist life is concentrated in the lower city (Gialós), the upper city (Chorió) is astonishingly quiet. Here, one can stroll for hours through narrow alleyways. The small *folkloric museum*, where the original interior of a manor house and costumes of the ancient inhabitants are displayed, is worth visiting.

Of all the sights on the island, the *Panormítis Monastery* is certainly the most famous. It is situated in a beautiful, secluded landscape in the extreme south of the island. The church originates from the 12th century and is decorated with very beautiful frescoes. The monastery is very large and offers accommodation for 500 persons, which is also necessary when on people from all over the Dodecanese make pilgrimages here during Pentecost and on November 8th. Apart from these times, the beds remain empty; however, during the main season, no cloistered silence can be found here because excursion boats bring hundreds of tourists to the island every day.

Symi / **Practical Information**

Accommodation

A-category: "Aliki" Hotel, Tel: 02 41/7 16 65.
B-category: "Dorian" Hotel, Tel: 02 41/7 11 81.
"Metapontis" Hotel, Tel: 02 41/14 91.
"Grace" Hotel, Tel: 02 41/7 14 15.
D-category: "Glafkos" Guest House, Tel: 02 41/7 15 21.
In addition there are numerous private rooms available. The rooms situated in the upper city are more quiet and usually also more reasonably priced. However, prices on Symi are generally relatively high. The following travel agencies rent out rooms, complete holiday apartments or houses:
"Sunny Land", Tel: 02 41/7 14 13.
"Symian Holidays", Tel: 02 41/7 10 77.
"Symiaki", Tel: 02 41/7 14 91.
Banks: There is a subsidiary of the National Bank of Greece on Symi.

Symi (Excursion) 114

Beaches: Symi is not exactly suited to swimming. One usually has to dive into the water, jumping directly from a rock. The only larger bay, which is situated at good walking distance from the town of Symi, is Pédi Valley about 3 kilometres (2 miles) from town. However, this has only a rather rough gravel beach.

All other bays on the island are only accessible by boat, for example *Nanoú Bay*, the island's most beautiful bay. Most boats leave the harbour around 10 am and return around 4 pm.

Restaurants: "The Trawler" Tavern near the city hall is not exactly cheap but the food is very good.

"O Meraklís" Tavern is somewhat hidden in the alleyways of the lower city and is certainly one of the most authentic taverns. Very friendly atmosphere.

"Giorgo's Tavern" is beautifully situated at the upper end of the Kalí Stráta (= good street), good Greek cuisine. Unfortunately, most of the taverns

The island of Symi counts among the most beautiful in the Dodecanese

at the Paralía have already adapted themselves to day-trip tourists, i.e. modest food for exorbitant prices.

Transportation:
Buses/Taxis: There is no bus service on the island which operates on a regular basis; only tour buses to the Panormítis Monastery are available. There are a handful of taxis on the island but these are rather expensive. Most of the bays for swimming can be reached via boat from the town of Symi

Ferries: Symi can be reached from Kos with the Dodecanese Lines (Kos — Symi — Rhodes); *(→ Kos City / Transportation).*

Important Adresses: The tourist information office is situated right at the clock tower on the harbour. This is also the location of the post office and OTE.

Telephones

As everywhere else in Greece, telephoning (and sending telegrams) is only possible at the OTE, an independent organisation responsible only for these two forms of communication. OTE is pronounced as one word with two syllables with a stress on the "e".

The OTE offices are usually open all day till late in the evening and quite often even during weekends *(→ individual entries / Important Adresses).* If a village is too small for an OTE office, there will always be a kiosk *(→ Períptero)* or a restaurant where phonecalls can be made.

One can dial the US, Canada and the UK direct but patience is often necessary until connection is established. Moreover, it can take up to half a minute until a signal can be heard; only try dialling again after hear ing a busy signal. Using the telephone in Greece is rather inexpensive by European standards: a three minute call to Central Europe costs around £3 ($5.65). The area code for Kos within Greece is 02 42, the internal code for Greece is 30 (leave off the zero in area code when phoning from abroad).

International Codes: United Kingdom — 0044; United States and Canada — 001.

Tílos *(Excursion)*

Tílos is easily accessible from Kos *(→ Kos City / Transportation)*. In order to adequately see and explore the island, several days must be planned into one's travel itinerary.

Tílos is one of the islands off the tourist track. Therefore, even in the main tourist season, only very few foreign tourists can be found here.

Particularly during the spring, a fine pink veil of almond blossoms blankets almost the entire island — a sight no one will soon forget.

There are two enchanting places to stay on the island — the harbour town **Liváda** offers diversity and beautiful, secluded sand and gravel beaches. A rather well preserved *abandoned village,* an abandoned *monastery* in the rugged mountainous landscape, and the *Charkadió Caves* where skeletons of the dwarf elephants were found. These animals died out around 50,000 years ago and until they were discovered some years ago, no one expected them in the Aegean region.

Although it is a very romantic island, Tílos suffers under severe problems from the population migration of this century. Meanwhile, there are only about 500 people still living on this island. Tílos is a rather poor island and most inhabitants live from agriculture. Holiday-makers should not expect too much comfort here and will certainly be rewarded by the hearty hospitality of the people.

Tílos / **Practical Information**

Accommodation

Most private rooms and guest houses are located in Livádia.

The island's second town, Megálo Chorió, is situated in the northern regions, several kilometres from the coast. Although more beautiful than Livádia architecturally, it also offers a few modest accommodation options.

Medical Care: There is doctor in Livádia.

Shopping / Money: It is possible to exchange money at the post office. Grocery stores on the island have an astonishingly broad selection of goods.

Sights: From the dilapidated castle above the town of Livádia, one can enjoy a beautiful view of estensive portions of the island all the way to the beautiful beach of Tílos, *Erystoú Bay*. North of town, in the rugged mountainous countryside, one will find the *Agíos Panteleímon Monastery*, the most important sight on the island. Every year on July 27th, the day of *Panteleímon* is celebrated here by the island's entire population.

Tourist Information: The island's information centre is the "Livádia" Hotel in the harbour town. People here are very helpful, with practical information at hand and will help when looking for transportation options.

Transportation: Tílos can be reached with the Dodecanese Line (Kos — Nísyros — Symi — Rhodes) (→ *Kos City / Transportation*).

There are only very few cars on the island, but the few private cars willingly take tourists to all important places for a fee.

Time of Day

Clocks in Greece are on Eastern European Time, two hours later than Greenwich Mean Time and 7 (New York) to 10 (Los Angeles) hours later than on the North American continent. In summer, the clocks are set an hour ahead at the same time as the rest of Europe.

Tingáki

Tingáki is a small village situated (like → *Marmáris)* on the northern coast; it has completely adapted to tourism.

With small interruptions, an endlessly long beach extends from Tingáki almost to Kos City. On many sections of the beach, the surf is very rough (→ *Beaches*). The beach is heavily frequented during the summer months. Moreover, Tingáki offers all the necessary tourist facilities for a carefree beach holiday.

Chains of hotels line the beach, taverns offer international cuisine with a Greek flair.

Tingáki could actually be a town anywhere at the Mediterranean since it completely lacks any distinguishing features.

Accommodation: Here too, large travel organisers have reserved most hotel capacity. Nevertheless, here is a small selection:

Tolári

A-category: "Tingáki Beach", Tel: 02 42/2 94 46-7, doubles priced between £23.50 ($44) and £33.50 ($62.50).
C-category: "Konstantinos Ilios", Tel: 02 42/2 94 41-2, doubles priced around £12 ($22).
C-category: "Sunset", Tel: 02 42/2 94 28-9, doubles priced around £13.50 ($22.50).
C-category: "Villa Andreas", Tel: 02 42/2 92 21, double-room around £10 ($19).
Transportation: There is a bus operating between Tingáki and Kos City several times a day.

Tolári

Tolári is a small village situated at about 5 kilometres (3 miles) east of Kardámaena. A very beautiful sand beach runs from → *Kardámaena* to this point so that in the high season, tourists can also be found here.

Tourist Information

All tourist information offices are run by the Greek centre for tourism (EOT). There is at least one office in all touristically relevant places. Here, one will find all kinds of information on the island, accommodation, services, brochures and booklets, current bus schedules and details on arrival and departure times for ships.

If on Kos for the first time, it is a very good idea to first pay a visit to the tourist information office in Kos City where one can obtain all the necessary information → *Kos City / Important Adresses*.

Traffic Regulations

Traffic regulations in Greece are more or less the same as in other Central European countries, although strict adherence to them is not necessarily a trait of Greek character. To many foreigners, traffic seems rather chaotic. Thus, a healthy portion of caution is highly recommended.

Without question, the most significant sight on Kos is the Asclepius Sanctuary with its Temple of Apollo

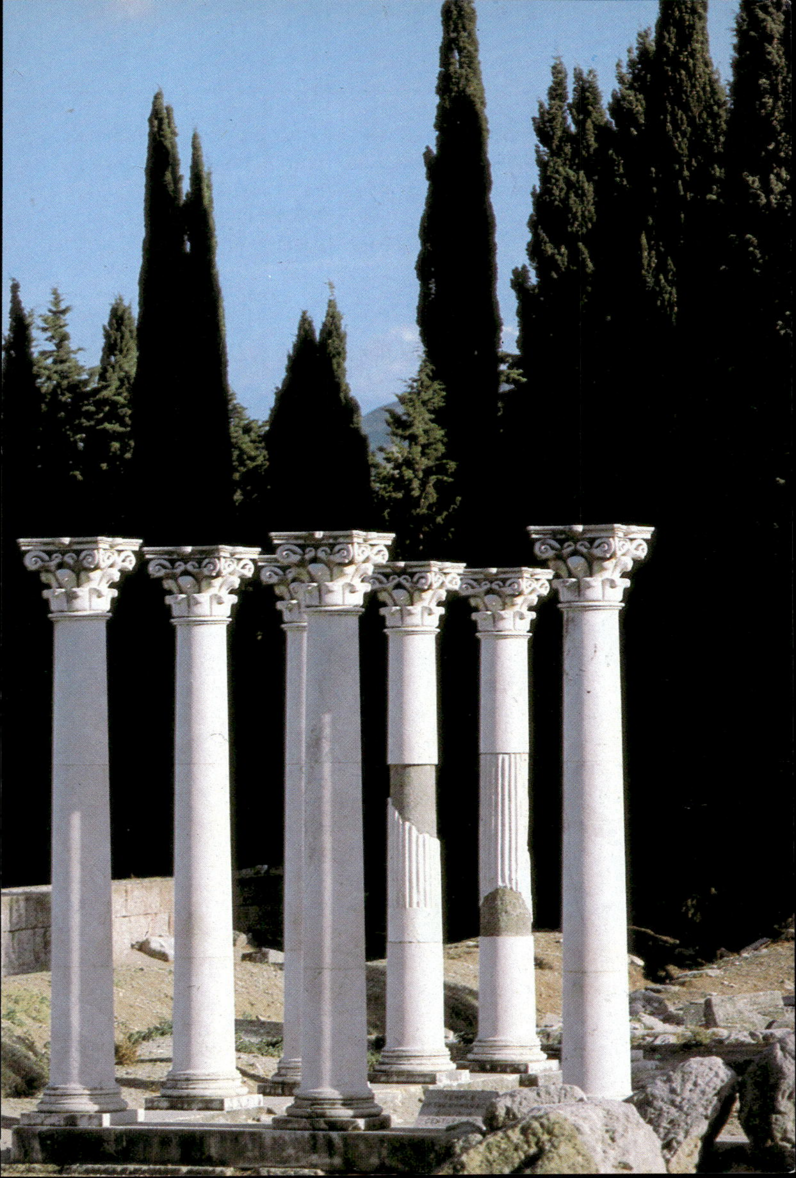

In the high season, one will find an especially large number of tourists exploring the island with motorcycles or bicycles. They constitute a risk themselves because many of them are on a motorcycle for the first time in their lives. So again caution and leaving them a generous amount of room are highly recommended (→ *Travel on Kos*).

Travel Documents

For a normal travel to Kos up to three month a normal *passport* is sufficient (→ *Visas*).

Children and young persons under 18 need their own passport or have to be entered in the parents' passport.

A *national driving licence* from one's home country is accepted in Greece but the *insurance papers* for the vehicle must be brought along. Although all Greek cars must have personal liability insurance, it is recommended to take out a temporary comprehensive insurance policy for one's own car since insurance claims with Greek insurance companies often entails substantial difficulties (→ *Car Rental*).

Furthermore, a *national identification sticker* must be affixed to the car.

No special *vaccinations* are necessary for travel in Greece.

Those who want to take their pet to Greece have to present *official certification of good health* for the animal. In addition, *proof of rabies vaccination* within the past 12 months must also be presented. The most practical way is to take along an international vaccination passport, filled out by the local authorities' official veterinarian.

Travel on Kos

Kos is very appropriate as "beach headquarters" in the central Dodecanese since the island is easily accessible.

By Car: A car is of course quite useful on Kos but not that necessary even if the island's network of roadways is good. Even though the island is around 40 kilometres (25 miles long), there are other ways to explore this island, especially when considering there is only one east-west traffic artery with auxiliary roads leading off to the coastal villages. All of the main roadways are paved.

By Bus: Kos' most important means of public transportation is the bus. Every village is connected with Kos City by the bus system; the frequency of buses is sufficient and the price is low (for example Kos City — Kardámaena 85p/$1.80). However, one will notice on Kos that the times the buses are in operation have not yet been completely adapted to the needs of tourists but are orientated toward the needs of the local residents (an exception to this is of course the excursion buses). So many of the buses operate in the early morning to Kos City and return in the afternoon. However, slowly but surely, tourists' interests are also being taken into consideration.

The bus terminal is in → *Kos City*. One can find out exact departure times here.

By Bicycle: Kos is one of those Greek islands which is exceptionally well-suited for cycling. There are no steep inclines and most streets run through a tuff plain. Astonishingly enough, there are numerous bicycle rental agencies on Kos even though this means of transportation is rather atypical for Greece.

By Ferry: The most important means of travelling to and from Kos is the ferry. Without this incredibly dense network of ferry routes, not only Kos but every other Greek island would be completely isolated and deprived of its basis of existence. The ferries are vital links for individual islands. Not only do they broung tourists but food, construction materials, spare parts, and even furniture. Starting from Kos, almost all other islands in the Dodecanese can be reached daily. There are ferries to the Eastern Aegean Islands and to the Cyclades and, of course, to Piaeus *(→ Kos City / Transportation)*.

Piraeus and Rhodes are accessible on very comfortable large-capacity ferries travelling at night — there is also an express boat to Rhodes. Moreover there are limited ferry connections with the Turkish harbour Bodrum (→ *Kos City / Transportation*). Information on prices, schedules, and other details are available at the EOT → *Tourist Information Office* in Kos City.

Ferry tickets are available at many travel agencies in → *Kos City* or even on the ferry itself, for those who decide on a trip on the spur of the moment.

Normally, a Greek ferry boat is divided into four classes: 1st, 2nd, and tourist class as well as 3rd class. Bookings for first and second class include use of a cabin; passengers in tourist class have a Pullman seat at their disposal, whereas those who book third class are only allowed to be on the open deck of the boat. Generally, third class passengers are also allowed to use the tourist class after all tickets are checked. Sometimes, the price for tourist and third class is identical. Only on the large night ferries to Piraeus and Rhodes are ticke chechs very strict and the adherence to the class booked is observed all night long. In this case, it is certainly useful to book a cabin because the journey takes 14 hours. There are usually enough cabins on the night ferries.

By Air: In addition to the international charter flights to Kos, there a good flight connections to other Greek airports (→ *Olympic Airways*).

The small international airport on the island is situated near the town of Andimáchia, about 25 kilometres (15½ miles) from → *Kos City*

By Motorcycle or Moped: The use of motorcycles and mopeds is much more recommendable than the use of cars. There are usually several rental agencies in every town. Here, some prices examples: a small moped costs around £4.35 ($8.15) a day; a moped up to 50 ccm, around £7 ($13). When renting for several days, a discount of 10% and more may be negotiated. Since there are not too many cars on the roads, the conditions for motorcycles and mopeds are almost ideal.

By Taxi: Those who like to be completely independent of bus schedules may of course take taxis, which is certainly the quickest way to reach one's destination. The minimum price for taxis in Kos City is 150 drachmas. It is, however, recommended to make sure the taxometer is set. Also, it is customary that the driver picks up additional passengers if their destination is on his way. Still, the passengers do not split the fare; everybody pays the full price for his or her route. Ordering a taxi by telephone is subject to a surcharge of around 65p ($1.25). The general prices are: base price around 65p ($1.25), price per kilometre around 13p (25¢). For longer trips, the price should be negotiated in advance.

Impressive bougainvilleas make for an intense and colourful contrast to the whitewashed houses

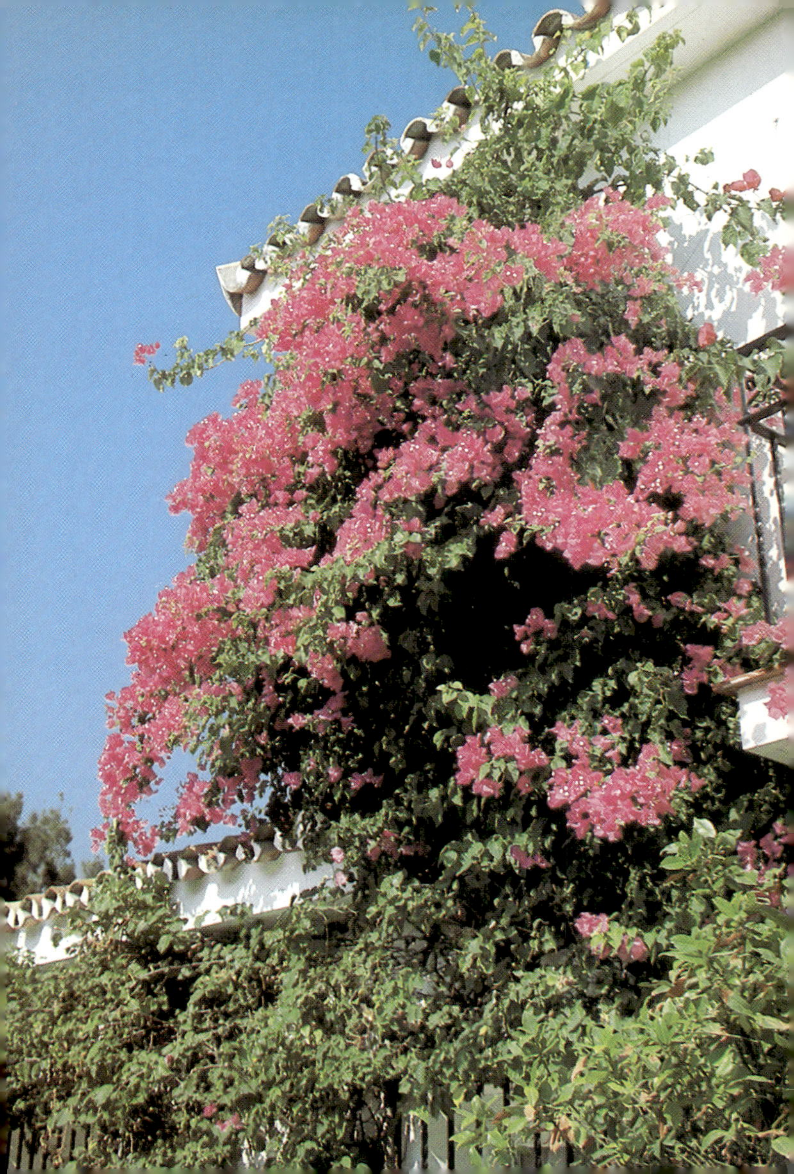

When arriving at the airport, the rule is: every taxi driver chooses his clients. The further the destination, the better the chance of getting a taxi. Taxi fare to Kos City or Kéfalos is around £7 ($13).

Travelling to Kos

By Car: Greece is presently only accessible in the practical sense by driving the route through Italy and taking a ferry, since the land route through former Yugoslavia is no longer an option and the route through Hungary, Rumania and Bulgaria cannot be recommended because of the poor road conditions, long waits at the borders and insufficient fuel supplies. This makes travelling to Kos from elsewhere in Europe by car not only expensive and time-consuming but not a very good idea in general since one can travel on and to Kos and its neighbouring islands very well without a car.

For the diehard drivers, some tips anyway for the route through Italy: the most important ferry harbours in Italy are Venice, Ancona, Brindisi and Bari. The three most important destination harbours in Greece are Igumenítsa, Pátras and of course Piraeus. When travelling during the high-season advance reservations will be essential since the ferries are filled to capacity. Only from Bari and Otranto could one have some luck in some cases and be able to travel without a reservation.

The duration of the journey depend on the departure point: Ancona —Pátras: around 35 hours; Bari — Pátras: around 20 hours; Brindisi — Pátras: around 20 hours. Since prices for individual passengers are calculated very differently, it is almost impossible to provide an overview here, therefore, an example is included: the trip from Ancona to Pátras costs from £50 to £80 ($94 to $150) for a passenger car and £24 to £134 ($44 to $250) per person.

By Bus: The Europabuses to Greece are also blocked by the problems in former Yugoslavia. Since the political development remains unclear, no information on this form of travel can be offered here until the situation changes.

By Air: Thus, the best, quickest and most convenient way to reach Greece and Kos is by air. Charter flights to Kos and Athens are offered from almost every major airport throughout Europe. Those who would enjoy a stopover in Athens can either take a continuing flight to Kos with Olympic Airways (several flights daily between Athens and Kos; airfare is around £30/$50) ot take one of the larger ferries from Piraeus to Rhodes. These depart daily and all dock at Kos. One drawback is that the ferry trip does take 14 hours.

By Ferry: The large car ferries between Piraeus and Kos operate daily and are quite comfortable due to their size. Most of these depart around midday from Piraeus and arrive on Kos around 4 am. The prices for the deck crossing ar around £12 ($22) per person; cabins start at £17 ($32) and £34 to £44 ($63 to $82) is charged for transporting a car.

Tickets for the ferries to Kos are best purchased at one of the many travel agencies along the harbour of Piraeus; prices are identical everywhere. The following are the addresses for the largest ferry lines in Piraeus:

— Agapitos Lines, Kolokotróni St. 99, Tel: 01/4 13 62 46.
— DANE, Astingos St. 4, Tel: 01/4 12 59 80.

Turkey *(Excursion)*

There are interesting possibilities to take a day-trip from Kos to Bodrum in Turkey *(→ Bodrum/Halikarnassós)*. However, be sure to take into account that package tourists in Greece are only allowed to undertake one-day trips to Turkey. Otherwise, Greek officials are entitled to declare the return ticket void when leaving the country. Therefore, one should ask for the exact current regulations which are valid for one's particular situation at the EOT before going onto such a trip. For example, in 1987 there was a decision by the Greek government intended to prohibit these trips completely. However, they are still carried out today and both sides are interested in this business which brings foreign currencies to both countries. And these trips are indeed quite expensive. The ferry alone costs more than £23 ($44).

Vegetation

Like most islands in the eastern Aegean Sea, Kos has abundant vegetation. Olive and lemon trees on the slopes of the → *Díkeos* as well as several types of pines and cypresses characterise the profile of the island. Especially in spring, Kos is, like many other island in Greece, virtually blanketed in an ocean of flowers consisting of poppies, wild daisies, hibiscus, oleander and jasmine — a sea of colour. The almond trees blossom, lending an almost impressionistic ambience to the countryside.

On the Greek islands, the contrast in vegetation between spring and summer is always striking. In May it is almost over: the flowers have dried, likewise the grass making a rather barren impression.

Only the Phrygána, small bushes and thorny underbrush endure. The Phrygána is even found in extremely rocky and dry areas. It grows everywhere where other plants had no chance of survival.

The vegetation on the slopes of the Díkeos Mountains almost resembles a forest. The following trees can not only be found on Kos but in the entire Aegean:

Beach pine *(Pinus maritima):* It grows very tall and has a cracked, reddish-brown. Its resin is used as a preservative in white wine, the retsina — a method that was already used in ancient times which lends the wines their characteristic and unmistakeable flavour.

Aleppo pine *(Pinus halepensis):* The aleppo pine has broad branches and reddish bark. The wood of this tree was predominantly used in ancient times in shipbuilnding. It is still used in construction today.

Black or Austrian pine *(Pinus nigra):* Very tall and recognisable by its grey and black bark.

Italian stone or umbrella pine *(Pinus pinea)*: Broad branches resembling the form of an umbrella and greyish bark characterise this tree which originally comes from Italy and is found scattered on Kos or in small groves.

Mediterranean cypress *(Cypressus sempervirens):* This type of cypress grows in form of a column when standing alone; otherwise with outstreched branches. It is a tree that was cultivated very early in Greece. The cypresses are often planted on cemeteries or near monasteries or churches since they are considered as symbols of enormous life forces. They live several hundred years.

Visas

Visas are not necessary for travelling to Greece unless planning to stay longer than three months. Twenty days before this period has elapsed, one must apply for a visa at the local police station. Generally, there are no difficulties if one makes a solvent impression and has adequate financial reserves (→ *Travel Documents*).

Weights and Measures

The normal Central European weights and measures (the metric system) are used in Greece as well. Only the metric pound is unknown, everything is measured in kilo. So a metric pound in Greek is "missó kiló" (½ kg). Open wine and olive oil are not sold in litres but in kilos as well, which all comes out the same in the end.

Wine

Cultivating wine has a long tradition in Greece that goes back far before Christ. With more than 600,000 tons of wine per year Greece is one of the largest wine producers in Europe even today.

Probably the most famous Greek wine and at the same time the most controversial is the Retsína. Retsína is a wine to which the resin of the beach pine is added as a preservative. Thus, the wine takes on its unmistakable and unique flavour which marks the parting of ways for many: either people love it or they hate it. In either case, it is a very agreeable wine. By now, however, numerous wines without pine resin can also be found.

Unfortunately, Kos is not such a famous wine island as her bigger sister Rhodes; most wines are imported to Kos. There are only very few homemade and self-pressed wines, usually produced by vinters for their own consumption.

Most red and white wines are quite dry and, therefore, make good table wines. The most famous ones come from Naoussa in Makedonia and from the Peleponnes (Deméstica).

Youth Hostels → *Accommodation*

Zía

Zía is one of the most beautiful mountain villages situated on the slope of the → *Díkeos*. Clean, whitewashed houses and small alleyways dominate towns profile.
Although Zía often serves as an example of a typical mountain village for many tourists, it is still astonishingly quiet. Most inhabitants of the village still make their living from agriculture which is the main branch of economy here.
The small shops in the village sell teas and other aromatic herbs, two small taverns at the Platía serve meals.
The "Sunset Balcony" Tavern in the village centre is very nice and offers a beautiful view of the coast, especially striking at sunset.
In Zía's other taverns, the famous and at the same time frightening "Greek nights" are organised for tourists. Excursion buses travel to these special taverns, but up to present, the village has not suffered under this form of tourism.
Those who are able to spend a holiday without a beach will probably find Zía a very pleasant place. From here, it is possible to climb the → *Díkeos*.
Accommodation: Up to present, only private rooms are available. There are no hotels. For more details ask at the taverns.

Zipári

Zipári is a small, insignificant village situated to both sides of a road about 10 kilometres (6 miles) from Kos City. It is here where to the road turns off to some of the mountain villages in the → *Díkeos*. The village even has a few taverns and smaller shopping facilities.
Transportation: Zipári has a bus to Kos City operating daily.